EPSOM
PAST

Epsom High Street, *c.*1930, before it was widened.

EPSOM PAST

Charles Abdy

Phillimore

2001

Published by
PHILLIMORE & CO. LTD.
Shopwyke Manor Barn, Chichester, West Sussex

ISBN 1 86077 180 7

Printed and bound in Great Britain by
BIDDLES LTD.
Guildford, Surrey

Contents

List of Illustrations

Frontispiece: Epsom High Street, *c.*1930

Illustration Acknowledgements

Mr. L. Bond, 39, 44, 64, 69, 70, 95-6, 106, 116, 125; Bourne Hall Library, 76, 83, 104; Bourne Hall Museum, Frontispiece, 8, 11-12, 17, 19-21, 23-31, 33, 38, 40, 41, 45, 46, 48, 54, 57, 59-62, 67, 68, 74, 77, 79-82, 84-9, 92-4, 109, 114, 115, 117, 118, 134, 136, 145, 146, 148-50, 154, 155; Mr. G. Cowlin, 103, 128, 131, 132, 135, 137, 138-41, 143, 144; Mr. J. Marshall, 37; Mr. J. McInally, 13; Mr. J. Norrington, 73; Mr. M. Runnells, 49, 52, 66, 71, 72, 101, 112; Surrey Archaeological Society, 2-5; Trades Union Congress, 156; The following are reproduced by permission of Surrey History Service: 122, 123, 151. The following are reproduced courtesy of Maryland Department, Enoch Pratt Free Library, 10, 147.

Unattributed illustrations are mostly from the author's collection. I have done my best to trace the owners of photographs that I have used: if I have missed any I apologise.

Acknowledgements

I am grateful to the many people who have helped me write this book and especially: the Librarian of W.S. Atkins (Services) Limited, for information on Woodcote Grove; the staff of Bourne Hall Library and the Surrey History Centre for their advice on tracking down old documents and for making them available; Andrew Cooper of United Racecourses Ltd for information on the Epsom Race Course; Graham Cowlin, who took many of the photographs of historic buildings reproduced in Chapter Twelve; Jeremy Harte, Curator of Bourne Hall Museum and his assistant, David Brooks, for making available so many old photographs and providing information on various aspects of Epsom, including schools; Geoff Howell, who working at Bourne Hall Museum, put together a file of information on the Second World War that I found of great value; the Rev. Michael Preston for information on St Barnabas Church; Ian West, Historic Buildings Consultant and acknowledged authority on the buildings of Epsom, who kindly read and commented on Chapter Twelve.

Finally, thanks to my wife Barbara, for her help in numerous ways.

Introduction

Gordon Home's *Epsom: Its History and Surroundings* was published in 1901, since when there has been no comprehensive narrative (as opposed to pictorial) history of the town. Sufficient has happened in the last 100 years to justify the publication of a new narrative history.

Home's history had its predecessors, notably Pownall's of 1825 and Swete's of 1860. The latter was written at a particularly interesting time, as the railways had arrived, and were beginning to have an impact. Actually, an event that would have had a greater effect on the lives of many people than the availability of trains was the provision of a public water supply and main drains that followed the damning report on the state of health in 1849. There is no reference to the prevalence of typhoid and cholera in Swete's chatty, gossipy account of an Epsom that seemed to be inhabited solely by the upper classes.

The book by Gordon Home is a remarkably evocative compilation, given that the author was only 23 years old, and it is good to know that he survived active service as a Major in the R.A.S.C. in the First World War and went on to make a name for himself as a writer and illustrator of topographical and historical books. As might be expected, the tone of the book is less sententious than that of the 1860 work which was written at the height of the Victorian religious revival. However, it cannot be said that it is overly concerned with social issues.

The world of 1901 was successful and confident: the new century was seen as expanding vistas of prosperity and progress. The young Gordon Home could not have imagined the horrors he would see in 14 years' time, horrors that were to be repeated a generation later.

Who knows what our new century will bring? Before it is too advanced it seems not a bad idea to set out a history of Epsom as it appears to an observer from the viewpoint of 2001. Surveying the past from this viewpoint, two prominent features have to be the growth of the spa following the discovery of the purgative waters, and the development of Epsom as the Mecca of horseracing in consequence of the overwhelming popularity of The Derby after it was initiated in 1780. These two events set Epsom apart from other Surrey towns.

Other than the effect of the two World Wars, the dominant feature of the 20th century was the growth in population as a result of the housing boom stimulated by improvements in rail services in the 1920s and '30s. Apart from the employment they provided the main effect of the complex of mental hospitals, the first of which had just been built when Gordon Home wrote, was that it kept open land that might otherwise have been used for housing development. Now, most of the hospitals are being demolished and replaced by housing estates.

There are so many facets to the history of Epsom that a detailed account would run to many volumes. What I have attempted to do is to set out the salient features and then elaborate on particular issues so far as the confines of the book will allow. Although the treatment is broadly chronological, some aspects are best dealt with thematically so that some overlapping of dates is inevitable.

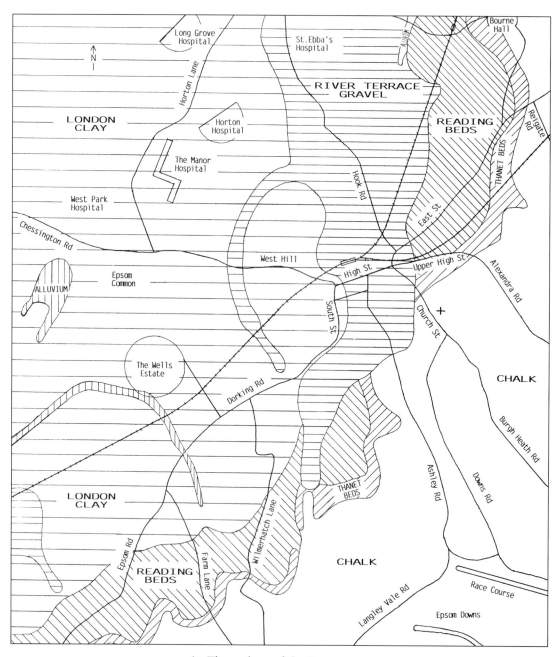

1 The geology of the Epsom area.

Chapter One

Epsom before Domesday

Prehistoric times

Epsom is on the spring line, where London clay and chalk are separated by the more porous Reading and Thanet beds. The centre of the town is in a bowl at an altitude of 60m and the land rises to a height of 155m on Epsom Downs, which have been described as a noble expanse of chalk country. About five kilometres farther south the summit of the North Downs is reached with an altitude of around 200m. This situation gave rise until recent times to a phenomenon called the Earth Bourne, an intermittent spring usually rising within a foot or two of the surface over a considerable area of Epsom, and occasionally oozing out above the ground. Sometimes it did not appear for three or four years, and then might flow for two or three years successively. It would last for a few months in the early part of the year.

The terrain would have favoured human activity in prehistoric times but the evidence is scanty: there are a few flints and arrowheads from the Neolithic period and from the Bronze Age a burial and a bronze palstaff. The Iron Age is represented by a couple of gold coins and a small amount of pottery. These finds were mostly from chalk or gravel areas: the heavy London clay was not popular for prehistoric settlement, although there is some evidence of a Late Bronze/Early Iron-Age settlement on the clay near the former Manor Hospital.

Roman period

When Roman times are reached, things are more interesting, with a late first-/second-century cremation cemetery, a tile kiln, pottery and a considerable number of coins. Just outside the Epsom boundary on Ashtead Common a

2 Hypocaust which was uncovered during excavation of the Roman bath house on Ashtead Common.

large complex of Roman buildings was excavated in the late 1920s consisting of a villa with some 13 rooms and an elaborate detached bath-house with hot and cold rooms and ante-chambers. Associated with the villa was a tile-works that made use of the local clay. Material unearthed indicated that the works produced flat bricks, roofing tiles, both tegula and imbrex, and box flue tiles. The villa complex was connected to Stane Street by a road more than three metres wide and some three kilometres long, more or less at right-angles to the major road, and suggests that the bricks and tiles would have been distributed to other parts of Surrey. Stane Street went through Epsom in a south-west direction, passing very close to St Martin's Church and across Woodcote Park. Box flue tiles carry various distinctive impressed patterns and a number of tiles found at Ewell had the same pattern as some of the Ashtead tiles. It is thought that the villa was constructed between A.D. 120 and 150 and came after the brick and tile works. Although these Roman remains are outside the Epsom boundary, Ashtead Common is a continuation of Epsom Common, and, since the Romans would have been unaware of present-day boundaries, this villa and tile works assume importance in relation to Epsom. The tile kiln referred to earlier was discovered during the construction of the West Park Hospital at Horton in 1922 and is considered to have been part of the Ashtead industry.

3   Roof tiles from the Roman Villa on Ashtead Common.

4   Box flue tiles from the villa stamped with 'dog and stag' pattern.

5 Suggested appearance of the Roman Villa and bath house in the second century drawn by R.T. Westendorp A.R.I.B.A.

The Saxons

Some time after the end of the Roman occupation of Britain in 410, the Saxons arrived, the colonisation probably being from the north down from the River Thames. An earlier spelling of Epsom had been Ebbesham, and the derivation is considered to be Ebbi's ham, i.e. Ebbi's homestead. The Saxon village is thought to have originated in the late sixth century or early seventh century as one of the numerous settlements that were established on the spring line and its location is likely to have been associated with the Roman road, Stane Street, since the parish church, around which the early village is assumed to have clustered, is very close to the route of the road. The parish that developed from Saxon times onwards was a strip parish some four miles from north to south and about two miles from east to west. The northern end is on London Clay, the centre including the original village is on the Woolwich and Thanet Beds and the southern end runs onto the chalk of the downs.

Epsom at Domesday

The Domesday Survey of 1086 shows Evesham (Epsom) as belonging to Chertsey Abbey and having 34 villagers, four smallholders, six slaves, 18 ploughs (each plough would have a team of six oxen), two churches and two mills. It was valued at £17 and would have been comparable in importance with Ewell, which was valued at £16. Ewell was owned by the King, but its church was on land belonging to Chertsey Abbey, and it is thought that the second Epsom church referred to in Domesday Book was in fact the Ewell church.

Chertsey Abbey

The Benedictine Abbey of St Peter was founded at Chertsey in 666. In a charter of *c.*675 Frithwald, the under-king of Surrey, granted the abbey extensive lands and there were further grants by later Saxon kings. The buildings were erected on a low-lying site on the banks of what is still known as the Abbey River, that joins the Thames a quarter of a mile north of Chertsey Bridge.

Towards the end of the ninth century the abbey was destroyed by the Danes and the monks were slaughtered, but it was refounded in 964 and went on to become one of the greater monastic houses, so that at the time of the Domesday Survey it held over 50,000 acres of land consisting of estates in Surrey and elsewhere.

Chertsey Abbey did well out of the Norman Conquest: William not only confirmed its possessions, but also granted it more land. However, when Abbot Hugh of Winchester took over in 1107 the abbey was in decline and he initiated a rebuilding programme that went on until the end of the 13th century.

Excavations carried out in the 1860s and the 1950s have brought to light a church 275 feet long and lined with Purbeck marble. The decorated floor tiles made by inlaying the pattern in white clay on the red earthenware body became famous and played a part in the revival of the encaustic technique in Victorian times when A.W. Pugin made some brilliant designs for Minton.

The tranquil life within the walls of the abbey came to an end at the Dissolution: the buildings were dismantled in 1537 by order of Henry VIII. It was a demolition so thorough that in the 18th century a Dr. Stukely wrote:

> Of that noble and splendid pile, which took up four acres of ground and looked like a little town, nothing remains, scarcely a little of the outer wall of the precincts. I left the ruins of this place, which had been consecrated to religion ever since the year 666, with a sigh for the loss of so much national magnificence and national history.

There is some doubt about the authenticity of the early Chertsey Abbey Charters, since they are available only in mid-13th-century copies, but certainly by the time of Domesday Book, Epsom manor was in the possession of Chertsey Abbey and there are many documents relating to it.

Chapter Two

Epsom and Horton Manors after Domesday

Epsom

The Epsom Manor remained in the hands of Chertsey Abbey until the Dissolution. Henry I granted the abbot leave to keep dogs on his land at Epsom, and to catch foxes, hares, pheasants and cats as well being allowed to take wood from the king's forests.

Two years before the manor was surrendered to King Henry VIII in 1537 it had been valued at nearly £21. The king granted it to Sir Nicholas Carew, who, as a young man, had been highly favoured and made Master of the Horse. Then, in 1539, Sir Nicholas was accused of involvement in a Papist plot and lost his head on Tower Hill. Henry took the manor back and made it part of the Honour of Hampton Court which was a large group of manors that included Nonsuch (Cuddington) and Ewell that Henry was putting together to form what was in effect a great hunting estate from the Thames down to Walton-on-the-Hill. The king's officers acted as stewards and bailiffs for the constituent manors.

In 1554 Epsom was restored to the Carews, when Queen Mary granted it to Francis, eldest son of Nicholas, who held it until his death in 1611. He had no son, and the manor came to the Darcy family and was eventually sold to Mrs. Anne Mynne, widow of George Mynne who had bought Horton manor. When Anne died, Epsom went to their daughter Elizabeth, along with Horton Manor, so Elizabeth was the owner of an estate comprising the two manors and which included Woodcote Park.

In 1648 Elizabeth married Richard Evelyn, brother of John Evelyn, the diarist. They lived at Woodcote Park, where Richard had a new mansion built to replace an earlier one. Richard died in 1670 and, until her death in 1692, Elizabeth ran the estate and the manorial courts were held in her name.

Elizabeth Evelyn had been granted by Charles II the right to hold a weekly market and two fairs at Epsom, a grant that was renewed in 1685 by James II. There was also

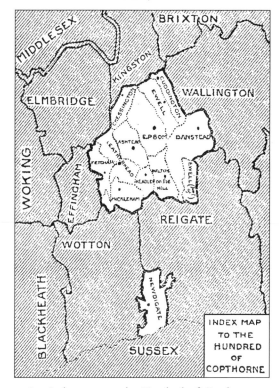

6   Index map to the Hundred of Copthorne.

5

7 Memorial to Elizabeth Evelyn (d. 1692) in Epsom parish church transferred from the old church. It has been described as 'a standard type but superbly carved'.

a grant to hold a court of pie-powder at each of the fairs. ('Pie-powder' is derived from 'piepoudrous' [*pieds poudreux*], 'dusty-footed', a term commonly applied to an itinerant trader, hence its association with a court held to administer justice among dealers at a fair.)

The patent roll for the grant starts by referring to an inquiry held by command of James II 'at the house of Mr. Clynch situated in Epsom in our county of Surrey on the twentieth day of May last passed'. (William

Clinch lived where Woodcote Grove now is.) This inquiry established that

> on the oath of respectable lawyers known in that county recently our brother Charles II granted to Elizabeth Evelin widow her heirs and assigns one market and two fairs to be held at Epsom ... a market in and upon any Friday in any week and the first of the fairs to begin in and upon the feast of St. Michael the Archangel and the second in and upon the feast of St. James the Apostle annually forever ... any such fair being about to last three days.

Further on, there is reference to power and authority being given to hold a market in Epsom 'in and upon each Friday in any week. Any profit advantage and emolument whatsoever, from tolls for stalls, fines and penalties, were to go to Elizabeth Evelin her heirs and assigns in perpetuity.'

On the death of Elizabeth Evelyn the estate was split up: Epsom went to trustees who held the courts until 1706 when John Parkhurst succeeded to the estate. It remained with the Parkhurst family until 1770, when it was sold off, after which the manor had a succession of owners. In 1818 the 'lord of the manor' was once more a widow, Mrs. Mawby, who gets the following mention in the Epsom Vestry minutes.

> Intimation has been given by Mr Lindsay, steward of the lady of the Manor, of her intention to appropriate all monies collected from the standing of Booths on the Downs during the Races and thereby depriving the racing funds of that support which it has enjoyed from time immemorial which is a breach of the privileges belonging to the inhabitants of Epsom and to which they conceive themselves fully entitled to from long custom and also from the herbage of the Downs being indisputably their property.

It would seem that the alarm of the Vestry was based on a misunderstanding, or perhaps the steward of the Lady of the Manor was being over-zealous, because a deputation from the Vestry that waited on Mrs Mawby and her

Trustees reported 'that they expressed much surprise, said they know nothing of the business and that they had given no such order and requested the collection might be made in the usual way and that it should be applied to the purpose it had been heretofore.' When, in 1913, Epsom Urban District Council wished to set up a Saturday market in Epsom, they became involved in negotiations with the Trustees of the then lord of the manor that resulted in an agreement that the council would lease the market for a period of three years at a yearly rent of £20 with an option to purchase the right of the Trustees for the sum of £500. The option was not taken up and the rights remained vested in the Trustees, whose agents arranged for the letting of pitches for stalls and the collection of rents.

Finally, the lordship of the manor was purchased by Epsom and Ewell Borough Council in 1955, by which time much of the land had been sold off. Since then the mayor is always lord of the manor.

The old manor house, Epsom Court, was detached from the manor in 1770, when it passed to the Revd. John Parkhurst and later became a farmhouse. It stood to the north of Epsom in what is now Pound Lane and gave its name to Court Recreation Ground.

Epsom Manor held two courts, the Court Leet and the Court Baron. The Court Leet was concerned with law and order and the regulation of the quality of food: it elected the Constables and the Aletasters. The Court Baron dealt with land-holdings and the services and rents due to the lord of the manor. Fortunately, court rolls going back to 1663, more or less the start of the Spa period, have survived and provide useful information on changes of occupation of sites.

Epsom had two large common fields to the south of the town, Smith Hatch and Woodcote to the east and west respectively of the Bittoms, which was an area of rough grazing in a steep dry valley. Smith Hatch is thought to have contained nearly 500 acres and Woodcote about 350 acres. The fields were divided into irregular areas called shots varying in size from a few acres to 50 or more, each one having a name, some of obvious derivation, such as Stoney Land, Withybed Corner or Long Ridge. Others less obvious included Lower Digden, Mackerell, Sullenden Bottom, Perle Hill and Wimble Hill. There were 25 shots in Smith Hatch Common Field and 24 in Woodcote Common Field.

The shots were sub-divided into strips, each of which had an area of about an acre or possibly half an acre, and these were cultivated by the manorial tenants, each of whom would have a number of strips scattered throughout the common fields to give a total holding of perhaps five or as many as 30 acres. This distribution ensured that the land was fairly shared with regard to quality so that one tenant should not have all the good land and another all the bad.

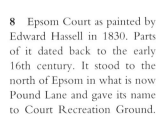

8   Epsom Court as painted by Edward Hassell in 1830. Parts of it dated back to the early 16th century. It stood to the north of Epsom in what is now Pound Lane and gave its name to Court Recreation Ground.

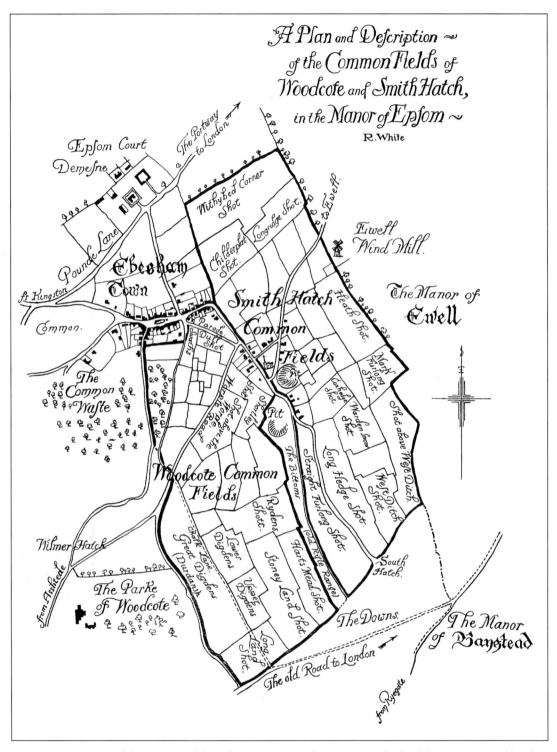

9 Conjectural map of the common fields of Epsom at an early date drawn by local historian Reginald White in the 1920s.

Horton

The land in the possession of Chertsey Abbey at the time of Domesday Book included what became the manor of Horton: it is not clear when the separation occurred. For much of the early period before the Dissolution the manor was held by members of the Horton family. Although their names occur in numerous deeds in Fitznell's Cartulary, little is known about them. (The derivation of Horton is said to be 'horh tun', dirty or muddy farm.)

In an early 15th-century charter, the manor owned by Chertsey Abbey consisted of the hamlet of Horton with 168 acres of land, 60 acres of pastures lying in the common fields of Horton, and various other properties including 100 acres of furze and heath in Ebbesham Common. In 1440 the abbot granted the manor to John Merton, the esquire of Henry VI, and his wife Rose, and their heirs. The king granted John and Rose free warren in the Horton lands and a licence to enclose 100 acres of land for a park. Rose outlived John, and on her death the estate passed through various hands and in 1626 was bought by George Mynne of Woodcote. At the same time George Mynne bought Brettgrave Manor, which had also originally been among the possessions of Chertsey Abbey. Brettgrave came to Mynne's daughter Elizabeth along with Horton and appears to have been merged with Horton.

When Elizabeth died, having survived her husband and children, she left Horton Manor together with Woodcote Park to Charles Calvert, third Lord Baltimore, to whom she was related. The first Lord Baltimore had married Elizabeth's aunt, Anne Mynne.

The sixth Lord Baltimore who inherited the properties left the country after a celebrated trial for rape in 1768 and sold the estates. Horton Manor changed hands several times and towards the end of the 18th century it was acquired by the Trotter family, several generations of whom held it. James, who succeeded in 1779, was High Sheriff of Surrey in 1798. His son John was M.P. for West Surrey in 1841-7 and he was succeeded by William S.Trotter. Horton Place was built by James Trotter and parts of its were incorporated in the administrative block of Manor Hospital.

Towards the end of the 19th century, the Horton Manor Estate was acquired by the Fowell Buxton family. By 1896, when it was sold to the London County Council who planned to build asylums there, it was somewhat neglected: the vendor, Sir Thomas Fowell Buxton, had gone to live in Australia.

10 Charles Calvert, 3rd Lord Baltimore, who inherited Horton Manor together with Woodcote Park from Elizabeth Evelyn, as painted by Sir Godfrey Kneller.

11 Epsom Parish Church, prior to its rebuilding in 1825, as drawn by Joseph Powell.

St Martin's Church

Both Epsom and Horton manors were in Epsom parish. It is generally considered that the present Epsom parish church stands on the site of a Saxon church, one of the two churches referred to in Domesday Book. The Saxon church was succeeded by a medieval building consisting of a nave with flanking aisles and a chancel. The porch was on the south side.

The medieval church, with the exception of the chancel, was rebuilt in the 15th century and a north-west tower, surmounted by a slim shingled spire, was added.

Chapter Three

The Spa

Until about 1620 Epsom was a small rural community with nothing to distinguish it, a much smaller place than nearby Ewell,which in 1618 had been granted a charter to hold a market. The discovery, by tradition in 1618, of water rich in magnesium sulphate, later known as Epsom Salts, was to lead to the rapid expansion of the village into a town as people began to come to take the waters.

The earliest known mention of the Epsom well is in 1629 when Abram Booth, travelling on behalf of the Dutch East India Company, described it as it was a few years after its opening: 'People coming there took a few glasses of the mentioned water—which has a taste different from ordinary water—after which walking up and down, these had in our opinion very good effect.'

Booth reported that many sick people came from far away places to drink the water and carry it away with them in bottles and jugs.

Samuel Pepys

People continued to take the waters during the Commonwealth period, but it was through the Restoration of Charles II in 1660 that Epsom became popular with the seekers of pleasure as well as the seekers of health. It was to be expected that the lively, inquisitive, fun-loving Samuel Pepys would have come to Epsom, and there are several references to his visits in his diaries.

On 25 July 1663 he rode out to Epsom with a friend, but, 'could hear of no lodging, the town so full; I went toward Ashtead, and there we got a lodging in a little hole we could not stand upright in'. His entry for the following day begins, 'Up and to the Wells'. Pepys drank two pots of the water which appeared to have a quick effect, and he observed how 'everybody turns up his tail, here one and there another, in a bush, and the women in their quarters the like'. (There were few facilities at the well on the Common in 1663.) He and his friend then walked through the town, greeting numerous citizens from London: he was surprised that many of them 'ever had it in their heads or purses to go to Epsom'.

On 27 July he was up in the morning about 7 o'clock and went again to the Common where he was entertained by an impromptu concert by a group of people singing. He drank three more cups of Epsom water before going for breakfast at Yowell (Ewell) before returning to London. Pepys went to his office the following day feeling more cheerful and refreshed.

For a visit in July 1667 he got up at 4 a.m. and was vexed with his wife for not being ready until after 5 o'clock. This time they travelled in a coach drawn by four horses and were able to take bottles of wine and beer and some cold fowl. They arrived at the well by 8 o'clock, and after Pepys had drunk four pints of the water to good effect they went into Epsom for a meal at the *King's Head*. In the afternoon they walked on the downs. Nell Gwyn was in the town at that time.

Nell Gwyn

Charles II began an affair with Nell Gwyn when he saw her on the stage of the Theatre Royal, 'in a hat of the circumference of a large coach-wheel, her little figure looking so droll that he was led to take her home in his coach to supper, and so to make her his mistress.' Nell had started at the Theatre Royal selling oranges, but she had a real talent for acting, particularly as a comic, and by the age of 15 she was performing on the stage. It was two years later that she caught the eye of the King. Samuel Pepys was captivated by the young actress and described her as 'pretty witty Nell'. There are frequent references to her in the famous diaries: he often saw her perform and spoke of her acting as being such as 'was never I believe in the world before'.

Pepys' diary for July 1667 reports that he put up at the *King's Head* (which stood where King's Shade Walk is now) where there was 'an ill room for us to go into, but the best in the house that was not taken up'. He goes on to say that, 'my Lord Buckhurst and Nelly are lodged in the next house, and Sir Charles Sedley with them: and keep a merry house'. The Countess of Warwick noted in her diary that, 'Nell and her two companions, and Sedley's young daughter, rode on the Downs, ate and drank and laughed the days away'. Nell Gwyn was 17 at the time, and not yet a regular mistress of Charles II. She became one of his favourites and one of her sons by him was made Duke of St Albans. (There is no evidence that Charles II came to Epsom with Nell Gwyn, although it is known that he dined at The Durdans in 1662.)

Charles' reputed last words, 'Let not poor Nelly starve,' seem to have been honoured and she was well treated by his successor, James II. Nell died at the age of 37 of apoplexy.

Shadwell's 'Epsom Wells'

Hearth Tax figures for 1664 show that Epsom (including Horton) had caught up with Ewell with regard to the number of chargeable house occupiers: a figure of 74 applied to both.

However, the number of hearths was higher for Epsom, 367 against 262 for Ewell, an indication that Epsom had more large houses.

By 1670 Epsom was so much frequented by Londoners out for a good time that playwright Thomas Shadwell wrote a play about it. The piece was a comedy entitled 'Epsom Wells' and it was first performed on 2 December 1672 at a London theatre in the presence of the King. He liked it so well that he saw it again two days later and, when on the 27 December it was performed at Whitehall, Queen Catherine also attended.

Compared with Congreve and Vanbrugh, Shadwell was not a great Restoration dramatist, but he was prolific, and popular in his day. It has been said that he gives a faithful picture of his age, roughly rather than finely drawn. Certainly, 'Epsom Wells' is noted more for its gutsy broad humour than for more subtle qualities. The plot is hardly profound: an assorted collection of London tradesmen and their wives, men about town, 'young ladies of wit, beauty and fortune', and a bumbling Country Justice, pursue amorous intrigues while taking the waters. The Justice, Clodpate, is made a fool of and tricked into a marriage with the 17th-century version of a gold digger.

It would be good to be able to report that this comedy of life in Epsom in the 17th century gives useful historical information about the town, but in fact there are few references to the buildings of the day. Although 'Epsom Wells' does not tell us much about the bricks and mortar of Epsom, it reveals a great deal about what people were up to and how they behaved. Shadwell's characters may not have been finely drawn, but they were blocked in with a sure touch in vivid colours, so that even a reading of the play beings them to life in all their lusty vigour. In the words of the Man of Wit, Rains, when rebuked for burning the candle at both ends, 'Is it not better to let life go out in a blaze than a snuff ?'

The picture painted is of Londoners coming to Epsom for a good time, making the most of the relaxed standards that came in with the Restoration. Perhaps the Epsom waters helped: maybe they were capable of more than cleansing the system! The behaviour was summed up by the observation of one character that, 'the freedom of Epsom allows almost nothing to be scandalous.'

The Well on the Common

The first Epsom Spa well was on the Common about a mile and a quarter to the west of the parish church. We have a record of what it was like in 1662 in the Journal of a Dutch artist, William Schellinks, who was travelling around England. He made a large drawing showing an undulating landscape with an open area surrounded by clumps of bushes and trees, in the middle of which is a small timber building. Groups of people stand around drinking the water, while some appear to be running towards the bushes. Schellinks gives a lively description of his visit in his Journal. He refers to Epsom as a famous and much visited place, very pleasant, The water was much drunk for health reasons, having purgative powers, and was sent in stoneware jars throughout the land. The well stood behind the small house in which there were some small rooms where people came to drink and also to shelter from the sun. The water was drunk on an empty stomach from stoneware jugs holding about one pint and some would drink 10 or even as many as 16 pints on a visit. Schellinks goes on to say that the water works 'extraordinarily excellent' which led to gentlemen and ladies putting down sentinels in the shrubs in every direction. He said that although Epsom village was fairly large, and could spread at least 300 beds, it was still too small and people were forced to look for lodgings in the neighbourhood.

Another useful eye-witness to Epsom Spa was Celia Fiennes, the indefatigable lady who travelled all over England on horseback between 1685 and 1712 and wrote up her experiences in her Journal. Her first visit to the well was some time around 1690, and she reported,

> It is not a quick spring and very often is drunk dry. To make up the deficiency people often carry water from common wells to fill it, which makes the water weak and of little operation. The well looked so dark and unpleasant, more like a dungeon, that I would not choose to drink it there. Most people drink it at home.

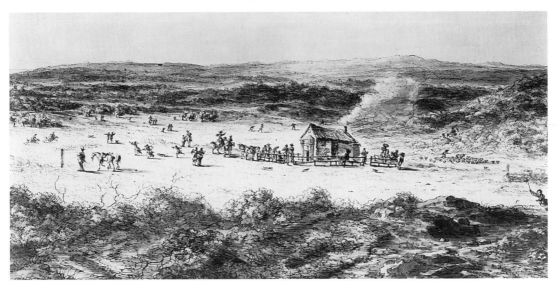

12   A drawing of Epsom Common in the vicinity of the Spa well, made by William Schellinks in 1662.

By shortly after 1700 the lord of the manor had taken away common land status from an area about 450 yards in diameter around the well and had had buildings erected for patrons, so on her second visit made in 1711 or 1712 Celia was able to say, 'Now the Wells are built about and there is a large light roome to walk in brick'd and a pump put on the Well, a coffee house and two roomes for gameing and shops for sweetmeats and fruite.' The circular area formed around the well has persisted and can be recognised in the layout of the modern housing estate that now surrounds the site of the well.

Richard Evelyn, who had been lord of the manor, died in 1670, and until 1692 his wife Elizabeth was on her own as lady of the manor. It has been suggested that there was a surprising lack of exploitation of the well in that period, and that the reason was the belief of the Evelyn family that Richard would have lived longer had he not drunk so much Epsom water: he had died from liver and kidney failure.

The Assembly Rooms (Waterloo House)

On the south side of Epsom High Street to the west of the Clock Tower stands a large red brick building long known as Waterloo House. It is in fact much older than the Battle of Waterloo: it was built in 1692 and did not get the name Waterloo House until after its days as spa assembly rooms. However, for convenience, I shall refer to it as Waterloo House.

Epsom had developed rapidly as a place of entertainment after the Restoration and by 1672 a bowling green had been laid out on what had been originally a field called Phillips Close, a three-acre pasture situated at the corner where the road to Leatherhead bends south at the junction of High Street and South Street. By 1692 the bulk of the three acres had been acquired by two London entrepreneurs, Michael Cope and Thomas Ashenhurst, and in the words of *Lloyds Evening Post*, 'About 1692 … magnificent taverns, the largest in England, were opened, public stands of sedan chairs and

13   The Assembly Rooms (Waterloo House) as they may have looked when first built in 1692 (drawn by John McInally).

14 Waterloo House in 1991. The building was unusual in having a through carriageway along its length.

numbered coaches were appointed, and Epsom became the most public resort of all ranks of people.' This is considered to relate to Waterloo House. Celia Fiennes described the building as having

> a very large roome with large sashe windows to the Green with cusheons in the windows and seats all along; there are two hazardboards; at the end is a Milliner and China shop this is belonging to the great tavern or eateing house and all the length of this roome to the streetward is a piazza wall (a colonnade), and a row of trees cutt and platted together as the fashion of the place.

The Spa Assembly Rooms consisted of front and rear ranges linked at each end by shorter ranges enclosing a central courtyard accessible through carriage entrances at each end. It is thought that such an arrangement with the carrriage way going from end to end is unique. It had two storeys, a basement and attics, and was built of red-brown bricks with stone quoins. The main front wall facing the High Street had a central section that projected two feet and was surmounted by a pediment. It was a fashionable style of building for the period and would have been designed by an architect. There were two long rooms in the rear range; an assembly room on the ground floor and a dancing room on the first floor. The front range had a coffee house and a tavern on the ground floor and a billiard room on the first floor. Behind the building was a bowling green and a cockpit. Many of the features of the spa assembly rooms can be seen in the present-day Waterloo House, although sadly the long rooms can scarcely be recognised.

15 *The Magpie*, since renamed *Symond's Well*, 1991.

The New Well

Shortly after the building of Waterloo House another entrepreneur, John Livingstone, began to exploit a well that had been sunk much nearer the centre of Epsom and which gave water having purging qualities similar to those of the water from the well on the Common. It was on land to the west of South Street owned by a Mr. Symonds near a public house long known as *The Magpie*, but which was renamed *Symonds Well* in 1996 in recognition of its past.

Livingstone was an apothecary who is thought to have settled in Epsom in about 1690. He had interests that included leasing the right to hold a weekly market and two annual fairs in the town. He bought property close to the new well and had a bowling green, gaming rooms and a dancing room constructed. An advertisement he had published in the *Daily Courant* of 8 April 1707 said:

> The new Wells at Epsom, with variety of Rafling-Shops, will be open'd on Easter Monday next. There are Shops now to be Let at the said Wells for a Bookseller, Pictures, Haberdasher of Hats, Shoomaker, Fishmonger and Butcher, with Conveniences for several other Trades. It is design'd that a very good Consort of Musick shall attend and play there Morning and Evening during the Season and

nothing will be demanded for the Waters drank there.

Livingstone acquired the lease of the old well on the Common, and on her second visit, in 1711 or 1712, Celia Fiennes wrote that on Monday there is

> raceing of boyes, or rabbets, or piggs; in the evening the Company meete in the Greenes, first in Upper Green, (Livingstone's complex) many steps up, where are Gentlemen bowling, Ladyes walking, the benches round to sitt, there are little shopps, and a gameing or danceing-roome; the same man at the Wells keepes it, sells coffee there also.

This is Livingstone's establishment at the New Well, and he is identified as being also the proprietor of the Old Well at this time. 'Then the company move to the Lower Green (Waterloo House Green) not far off, just in the heart of the town, its a much neater Green and warmer.'

The Old Well appears to have been closed shortly after the visit by Celia Fiennes. At times Livingstone has been vilified for shutting it down, but, given the greater convenience of the new well nearer the centre of the town, it would make commercial sense to concentrate his operations there.

The Spa at its peak

With the opening of Livingstone's buildings in 1707, Epsom Spa reached the height of its popularity. A regular coach service from London had been established in 1684, making it easier for Londoners to visit the Spa. With two entertainment centres in the heart of the town and one around the old well on the Common, visitors were well catered for. The free thinker, John Toland, who lived in Epsom for a number of years following 1710, has left a vivid description of life there in his 'Letter to Eudoxa' first published in 1711. (For more about Toland see Chapter Thirteen.) The description is written in a consciously high-flown poetic style, but does provide interesting information, and the work justifies making the following quotations: some of the more flowery passages have been omitted.

> Epsom ... much frequented for its most healthy Air and excellent mineral Waters ... It is deliciously situated in a warm even bottom, between the finest Downs in the world on the one side (taking their name from the village of Bansted seated on their very ridge) and certain clay-hills on the other side, which are variously chequered with woods and groves of oak, ash, elm and beech, with both the poplars, the intoxicating yew and the florid white-beam ...
>
> ... the houses of the very Townsmen are every where mighty neat, built most of 'em after the newest manner, and extremely convenient, being purposely contrived for the entertainment of Strangers, and therefore beautify'd by the owners to the utmost of their ability. The fronts are adorn'd thro'out with rows of elm or lime-trees, in many places artificially wreath'd into verdant Porticos ... The finest of 'em all is that which shades the pav'd Terras in the centre of the town, extended quite along the chief Tavern and Coffee-house.
>
> The two rival Bowling greens are not to be forgot, on which all the company by turns, after diverting themselves in the morning according to their different fancies, make a gallant appearance every even, (especially on Mondays) musick playing most of the day, and dancing sometimes crowning the night.

> The Ladies, to show their innate inclination to variety, are constantly tripping from one green to the other: and the Men are not more sure to follow 'em, than glad of the occasion, to excuse their own no less propensity to change.
>
> ... I must do our Coffee-houses the justice to affirm, that for social virtue they are equal'd by few, and exceeded by none, tho I wish they may be imitated by all. A Tory does not stare and leer when a Whig comes in, nor a Whig look sour and whisper at the sight of a Tory.

Other comments by Toland suggest that the happy atmosphere in Epsom could be attributed to a 'Master of Ceremonies' who was active in promoting the interests of the town.

It is significant that Toland has much to say on the social life and the rural delights, but says nothing about drinking the waters. It would appear that most people went to Epsom for 'the diversion ... the mirth and the company, rather than for the 'physick', to quote from Daniel Defoe, who added 'the nobility and gentry go to Tunbridge, the merchants and rich citizens to Epsom ...'.

Hare coursing was a popular entertainment for visitors. A hare warren on Walton Downs is said to have been set up in 1720 by the fifth Lord Baltimore of Woodcote Park and some of the wall still stands to a height of eight feet or so. The hares bred in the enclosure would have been driven out through small trap doors in the wall onto the downs to be chased by dogs.

16 The wall of the hare warren that was built on Walton Downs in 1720.

17 The Old Well House incorporating the remains of the long room that was built over the well on the Common as pictured in 1796.

The decline of the Spa

Epsom stopped drawing the crowds soon after the end of the first quarter of the 18th century. In 1738 Defoe was referring to its loss of reputation which he said could be attributed to its nearness to London: the gentry preferred to go to places that attracted less dubious characters.

There was strong competition from other spas, particularly Bath and Tunbridge Wells which, together with many other places, had more copious supplies of mineral water than did Epsom. In her visit to the well on the Common, Celia Fiennes had remarked on the poor flow. Also, it may be that the waters of some spas are less unpalatable than Epsom water, which is particularly bitter.

It has been suggested that the loss of the enterprising spirit of Livingstone on his death in 1727 marks the beginning of the decline. Another factor could be that chemists started producing Magnesium Sulphate, which gives Epsom water its purging qualities, from various sources, and when it became available 'over the counter', those who came to Epsom for purely medicinal reasons would not bother to do so.

There is a further explanation, which, so far as I know, has not been explored in depth: the development of pleasure gardens in London in the 18th century. Although Vauxhall Gardens in Lambeth opened soon after the Restoration in 1660, it was not until they were taken over by a new manager in 1728 that they really developed as pleasure gardens. They were soon offering a wide range of entertainments, with supper rooms and nightly musical entertainments. The grounds were lit with 1,000 glass lamps. Although the entrance fee of one shilling was sufficiently modest not to deter any but the very poor, the wealthy were not ashamed to be seen there, and the gardens attracted a wide range of social classes.

Ranelagh Gardens, next to Chelsea Hospital, opened in 1742. They had a great amphitheatre, the Rotunda, where concerts were performed and tea was served in the tiers of boxes that lined the walls. Masked balls were held and there were firework displays. Ranelagh soon became even more popular than Vauxhall. There were dozens of smaller, less fashionable pleasure gardens around London. With such amusements available in the capital, for many within walking distance of their homes, why should Londoners more interested in pleasure than health take an expensive and uncomfortable coach ride out in the wilds of Surrey? In fact, for those who were concerned with their health, there were numerous mineral springs and wells in London, including those at Lambeth, Tottenham Court and Islington.

An interesting glimpse of Epsom at about the time its popularity began to wane is provided by the replies made by the vicar to the questionnaire that preceded the Bishop's Visitation of 1725. He supposed the population to be 1,500 souls. Each year there were six marriages, 60 births and 50 burials. There were no Papists but there was a meeting-house of the Presbyterian sect. The names of the noblemen and other gentlemen of the parish included Lord Yarmouth, Lord Guildford, Lord Baltimore, Sir John Ward and numerous esquires.

Chapter Four

The Epsom Vestry 1770-1894

By the 17th century Parliament had made parish vestries responsible for matters such as the upkeep of local roads and bridges and the care of the poor and orphans as required by the Poor Laws and vestries eventually took over most of the functions that had been exercised by the manorial courts. The minutes of the Epsom Vestry are available from 1770 onwards and throw light on the life of the post spa town during that period. The minutes were for the most part clearly written in a copper-plate hand by the vestry clerk: in 1771 he was being paid four guineas a year. Most of the Vestry meetings started in the church on a Sunday and were adjourned and continued some days later elsewhere, usually at 6 o'clock in the evening. Early minutes refer to Mr. Morris's Coffee-house, but by 1776 *The Spread Eagle* was the venue and later many other Epsom inns are mentioned. For a period from 1800 to 1815 the meetings were held in a room that had been fitted up for the purpose in the Poor House.

Membership of the Vestry

The Epsom Vestry appears to have operated as a 'Select Vestry', i.e. consisting largely of self-appointed men of substance. They included William Northey, who was lord of the manor of Ewell, Cheam and Cuddington. There was also Joseph Shaw Esq., who was a J.P., the Rev. Dr. Madan and Sir Mark Parsons.

Occasionally a public meeting would be called, as the one on 2 October 1797 at *The Kings Head Inn* to consider the accounts of the Surveyors of the Highway.

At most meetings the two churchwardens were present. They would have been appointed annually for a one year term of office. The churchwardens had considerable responsibility for maintaining the church and running the parish: they also looked after the accounts. It has been said that churchwardens were the very foundation of democratic local government in England. They were unpaid, and understandably the job was not a popular one: however, suitable parishioners were expected to take their turn at it. There is an interesting entry for 2 December 1773 concerning Mr. Batchelor, one of the church-wardens in 1770, who had ignored several notices to attend the Vestry. The current churchwardens were instructed to remove and examine his accounts and report at the next meeting. On reading this, one feared that Thomas Batchelor would be found to owe money to the parish, but no, when the accounts for 1770-1 were checked, it was found that he was owed £25 5s. 2d. by the parish!

The rates

One of the important functions of the Vestry was to agree the rates needed to raise the money required for the relief of the poor, the main-tenance of the church and to cover the various other expenses that could be incurred by the parish. The poor rate could vary considerably

18 Epsom, from John Roque's map of Surrey, 1768.

0   0.5   1.0   1.5   2 Miles

From John Roque's map of Surrey, 1768

Original scale 2 inches to one mile

The map was oriented to the Magnetic North

Approx.
True North

19   Epsom *c.*1790, from a coloured pen and ink drawing.

from year to year, depending on economic conditions and the number of people unable to make ends meet.

On 18 June 1772 the poor rate was fixed at 2s. in the pound. It rose to 2s. 6d. in 1773 and by 1797 was 3s., rising still further to 4s. in 1801, presumably as a result of economic problems arising from the Napoleonic Wars. Although by 1807 the poor rate had been brought down to 2s., complaints that that was too high led to the appointment of a 'Rates Officer' to collect the rates and organise relief. This appears to have had an effect, as later in 1807 the figure came down to 1s. 6d. at which it remained until 1809 when it rose again to 2s.

People were no more anxious to pay their rates in the days we have been considering than in more recent times; defaulters were a recurring problem and were frequently listed as such in the Vestry minutes. On 16 May 1800 a meeting had to be adjourned because there were so many defaulters that the Overseers' accounts could not be completed.

The church maintenance rate was made as necessary to keep the church in repair and could vary from a few pence to as much as 1s. 6d. At times rates had to be set for special purposes, an instance being the rate of one shilling in the pound agreed on 18 December 1796, 'to defray the expense incurred in raising Volunteers for His Majesty's Army Levied by a Late Act of Parliament'.

The administration of the Poor Laws

The duties of the Vestry in respect of the care of the poor and orphans were sometimes carried out by overseers of the poor appointed by the Vestry, while at other times the work was farmed out to contractors after competitive tendering. At a meeting on 12 August 1771 the proposals of a Mr. Townsend and a Mr. John Bulley 'to maintain and take care of the poor of this Parish' were considered. John Bulley had proposed to take on the job for a term of three years in return for a payment of £440 a year and this tender was accepted.

20   The Poor House, Epsom, in 1829, as painted by Edward Hassell.

In 1777 the job of caring for the poor was being advertised in public newspapers, and on 12 September John Evans was appointed for six years. He undertook to erect a workshop and a stable for a horse. It would appear to have been an ill-advised appointment: when a Vestry committee reported on the workhouse in 1779 they found children in a state of near nakedness, dirty, lousy and in a very wretched condition, and the older people were in much the same way.

> We tasted the beer and the old people declared that instead of it being bittered with hops, it was bittered with feverfew and we think the same. We found a lunatic partly naked and chained. The children said they were not taught to read. We found the house so very offensive above stairs that we could not go to inspect the rooms and bedding.'

It was agreed that John Evans should forfeit £200 of his payment for breach of contract and that action should be taken to remove him. He was not prepared to go quietly, and his counterclaim was still in dispute two years later.

In 1793 a Mr. Harris was the 'contractor for the maintenance of the poor', and he proposed that some boys in the workhouse should be sold to the Marine Society in order to be sent into the Sea Service and that several girls should be apprenticed to a cotton manufactory at Carshalton. These proposals were rejected.

'Selling' children was under consideration again in 1805 when an item on the agenda for a Vestry meeting was to consider the propriety of placing some of the children out to a manufactory. The factory in question was a cotton mill at Iver near Uxbridge that had been advertising for children aged from 10 to 14 years old. Some members of the Vestry queried whether they could be accepted a year under 10 or more than 14, 'there being now about 10 of each in the workhouse which they wish to put out'. The matter progressed to the extent that members of the Vestry went to inspect the factory. At a subsequent meeting it was reported that, 'further enquiries have shown that there are reasons for supposing that the Employment in a Cotton Manufactory may be prejudicial to the Children's Health' and consideration was postponed. In April 1806 a request by a Mr. Merryweather for some poor children for his factory at Otley in Yorkshire was rejected unanimously. Although the proposals for 'selling' children to factories seem not to have been accepted, apprenticeships were another matter and were encouraged.

At a meeting in September 1800 it was, 'Resolved by a very great majority that the poor in the Poor House shall continue to be under the management of two persons to be appointed by the Parish under the inspection of the officers for the time being and a committee and not let to Farm.'

The master of the poor-house in 1812 must have been a particularly worthy man, because it was 'Resolved that the Overseers do make Edward Coxon the master of the poor-house a present of £5 5s. 0d. at Christmas next for his good management and conduct as master of the same.'

The wide range of matters dealt with by the Vestry can be illustrated with a few examples:

4 May 1803: Mr James B ... promises to pay the Overseers of this Parish the sum of fifteen pounds in six months from this day on account of Sam. R ... as a compensation for a Bastard Child sworn to him by Mary A ... [The idea behind the CSA is nothing new!]

8 November 1812: [There was discussion of] The expediency of providing a school for the education of the children, male and female, of all the poor inhabitants willing to benefit by it, in the principles of the Established Church and that a voluntary annual subscrip-

tion of the inhabitants be solicited for the maintenance of it.

18 May 1818: [A Beadle was appointed at a salary of 10 guineas a year, the parish to furnish him with] A greatcoat and a hat once in two years, a pair of shoes and a pair of stockings every year.

22 April 1847: It appearing that the keeping of the Town Pond in repair is attended with a great expense to the parish and that its stagnant water is exceedingly prejudicial to the health of the inhabitants, resolved that the Surveyors be requested to adopt measures for filling up the pond and for making a sewer along the centre of it.

(It is of interest that the filling of the town pond was under consideration as early as 1847, i.e., two years before the official report on the poor state of sanitation in Epsom.)

The Poorhouse/Workhouse

The Workhouse was originally known as the Poor House, but as legislation came in that made it necessary to set the poor to work, the term 'Workhouse' became more appropriate, although throughout the period covered by the Vestry minutes, both terms were used at different times to describe the building that had been built on the Dorking road behind which the

21 The Almshouses were built in 1703 by the entrepreneur John Livingstone on a piece of land in East Street granted by the parish. This picture was drawn by Yates in 1825.

Union Workhouse was later built. The Epsom District Hospital now occupies the area.

On 18 November 1778 it was agreed that

> a Mrs R ... was to be transferred from a mad house at Hoxton where she has been for several years, to Epsom Workhouse. She was in a quiet state of mind, not outrageous at any time but was in a melancholy state.

On 4 March 1801 it was stated:

> In consequence of the crowded state of the Poor House and many of the Poor being afflicted with the Itch and which continues to spread among them, the Churchwardens and Overseers be desired to look out for some proper place for the purpose of separating those who are in good health from those who are infected with the above or any other disorder that may require their being removed.

The Vestry had the employment of the poor in mind in November 1800 when they were seeking to elect, 'a man and his wife to superintend the internal management of the Poor House and to instruct the Poor therein in some useful Manufactory'. Straw-work and sack-making were considered suitable occupations.

Epsom had almshouses as well as the Workhouse and on 29 October 1772 the relationship between them was spelt out: 'All people under 50 living in the Almshouses must remove from them in a fortnight's time. If they do remove they will be sent to the Workhouse. In future no one under 50 shall be allowed in the Almshouses unless the Vestry gives specific consent.' (The almshouses had been built in 1703 by the entrepreneur John Livingstone for 12 poor widows on a piece of land in East Street granted by the parish. They were rebuilt on the same site c.1866.)

There is a glimpse of the diet of the poor in the minute of 30 March 1803 which states: 'Mr Radford, Mr Charman and Mr Hope to serve the poor house with Clods and Stickings of good beef at 3s 2d per stone', and on 9 May 1811 it was 'Resolved that the complaint of the poor respecting the quantity of meat is frivolous'.

At some periods the discipline imposed on the poor seemed particularly harsh, as in 1812, when it was, 'Resolved that no pauper in the poor house shall leave the House without leave of the Master and then not without a ticket and if anyone be found about the Town without a ticket such person shall be allowed bread and water only for two days after such an offence.'

A minute of 18 December 1818 reveals that the Rev. Douglas was a thoughtful man: he not only made a handsome present of 12 testaments for the use of the poor in the Poor House: he also provided 12 pairs of spectacles!

Outside relief

Although the major relief provided for the poor was by way of the workhouse, some help was given to needy parishioners who were not in the workhouse. This included a payment of 2s. 6d. per week to Mrs. S ... for the keep of a child belonging to William D ... and payments to men when their wives were ill. Payments to William B ... were dependent on his marrying Maria T ..., a widow with four children. Payments were also made to enable needy boys to become apprentices.

The militia and the army

Each county had to provide a certain number of militia men and each parish had to make its contribution. The men were chosen by ballot: they could avoid service by paying £10 for a substitute.

The invasion threat from Napoleon in the heyday of his career from 1803 to 1805 led to the formation of an 'Army of Reserve' of 50,000 men selected by ballot. The danger was imminent: the Grand Army was encamped at Boulogne equipped with flat-bottomed boats for the invasion. The Epsom Vestry called a meeting, 'for the purpose of appointing overseers and officers for removing of the livestock and other stock in this Parish in case of invasion.'

Surrey did not meet its target of 1,781 men for the Army of Reserve and a fine of £20,200 was imposed, spread over all the parishes, and this explains the entry in the Vestry minutes for 21 April 1805, 'The fine laid on the Parish under the Defence Act, £28.5.0 is so small that a rate cannot conveniently be made to defray it.'

The invasion threat was brought to an end by Nelson's victory at Trafalgar in 1805.

The Vestry and St Martin's Church

The Vestry could be quite eloquent: when Mrs. Trotter of Horton Place made a present of 'two very handsome Suits of Rich Crimson Velvet for the Pulpit and Altar', a letter was drafted expressing, 'warmest thanks for the very handsome manner in which you have ornamented our Church. Our pleasure in seeing its former Nakedness and meanness rendered thus perfectly neat and elegant is much enhanced by the Reflection that we owe it to the unsolicited Munificence of one of our own Parishioners.'

The church that the Vestry was responsible for had been rebuilt around the middle of the 15th century when the tower had been erected. Repairs were frequently needed. In the early 1820s there are references to a bigger church being required. A surveyor reported in 1823 that a moderate annual expenditure would keep the existing building in repair, and the fabric would withstand an extension: however, he recommended that it would be better to build a new church at the cost of £10,000. This proposal was accepted and an entry for 21 August 1825 states that the rebuilding had been completed: the expenditure exceeded the estimate by nearly £2,000. (How familiar that is!)

22 The old church contained a number of memorials by the celebrated sculptor John Flaxman. This is Flaxman's memorial to John Warre, produced in 1801. It was transferred to the new church.

Charities

Epsom was well provided with charities and on 15 November 1772 it was decided that, 'A summary of the various charities that have been left to the Parish of Epsom shall be drawn up and written on black boards in gold lettering and placed in various conspicuous places in the Parish Church.' Charities referred to in the Vestry minutes include those provided by the following benefactors: Mr. Brayne, Mrs.

Cullerne, Mrs. Mary Dundas, Mrs. Elizabeth Evelyn, Mrs. Elizabeth Northey, Mr. David White, Mr. Wright.

An open Vestry was held annually on the first Sunday in September to, 'enquire into the distribution of the different Charities belonging to this Parish'.

The bequests took a variety of forms: Mrs. Elizabeth Evelyn had provided for six poor women to be clothed at Easter. On 6 October 1800 it was reported that those benefiting had been given: 'One Grey Lindsey Gown and Coat, two shifts, one pair of Dark blue woollen stockings, one pair of strong shoes and one blue and white Checked Apron.' A note said, 'If none of the six women who are cloathed Die before the third year, they are entitled at that time to receive the charity again.'

David White's charity started in 1725. By 1802 the fund consisted of £3,384 in South Sea Annuities and produced an annual dividend of more than £101, a considerable sum at that time. However, in 1807 it was reported that 'Mrs. Cullerne's charity has been unproductive this year'.

The decline of the Vestry

In much the way that Vestries had taken over many of the functions of the manorial courts, so in their turn Vestries lost their powers with the setting up in the 19th century of administrative bodies not connected with the Church. The Poor Law Act of 1834 aimed to make the relief of the poor more efficient by grouping parishes into large districts known as poor law unions. The large Union Workhouses replaced the multitudinous parish workhouses.

Epsom was the largest parish in the group of more than a dozen parishes brought together to form the Epsom Union. A union was run by a board of guardians elected by the parish vestries and ex-officio justices; for the first meeting of the board in 1836 Epsom returned three guardians, Henry Milles of independent means, William Butcher a builder and Thomas Whitbourne a farmer. Baron de Teissier as senior magistrate presided. At the second meeting it was agreed to build a central workhouse for 300 persons at Epsom on land to the rear of the old poor house in Dorking Road.

The board laid down the uniform to be worn by the inmates of the new workhouse which included striped calico shirts for the men and boys, blue print or striped gowns for women and striped frocks for girls, with of course all other necessary garments.

Responsibility for public health was taken over by a Board of Health and in 1853 it was insisting that a permanent supply of good water must be made available in Epsom. The Vestry were not too happy with some of the Board's demands and it led to a complaint that they were interfering improperly in the duty of the Board to enact the law! (A report of 1849 had strongly recommended the provision of a good water supply and the need for sanitation.)

Towards the end of the 19th century the matters discussed are largely confined to those relating to the running of the Church. There was on several occasions unseemly squabbling over the allocation of pews. The Local Government Act brought about the setting up of the Epsom Urban District Council in 1894 which brought to an end the Vestry as an organ of local government.

Chapter Five

The First Half of the 19th Century

After the decline of the Spa, Epsom sank so much in importance that in the early years of the 19th century it was being described as a village rather than a town. Farming was almost medieval, with common fields that were divided among the villagers; the parish was not enclosed until 1869, and its enclosure was one of the last in the country. (Neighbouring Ewell had been enclosed in 1802).

Coaching Days

Apart from the occasional influx of visitors on race days, the greatest excitement in the early days of the century would have been the arrival and departure of coaches at *The Spread Eagle* and *The King's Head*. The day started with the departure of Hunt's two-horse Epsom to London coach from *The Spread Eagle* at 8 a.m. and a further seven coaches picked up passengers

23 *The King's Head* was one of the early spa-period inns. In 1838 the front was extended to create an assembly room on the first floor which became a popular meeting place.

24 *The King's Head* assembly room shortly before the building was demolished in 1957.

for London throughout the day until 4.30 p.m. These were four-horse coaches starting from Dorking, Horsham, Guildford, Worthing or Bognor Regis. The journey time from Epsom to London, Holborn, a distance of 17 miles, was 2½ hours. 'The Comet' coach went from Bognor Regis to London via Epsom, 66 miles in 8½ hours, with a number of changes of the teams of horses along the route. The horses were worked hard and would be worn out in two or three years. There were services in the opposite direction throughout the day from 11.00 a.m. to 6.00 p.m. followed by the arrival of Hunt's Epsom service at 6.30 p.m.

Reviving Fortunes

The 19th century saw a revival in the fortunes of Epsom as the growing popularity of the Derby brought more visitors to the town. In 1824 the churchwardens and a building committee entered into a contract with a London builder for the building of a new church in the Commissioners' Gothic style and this was completed in 1825 as a simple construction similar to the medieval one: an aisled nave and a chancel. It was built of flint with Bath stone dressings, and these materials were used to dress the old tower which was retained. The opening of the Grand Stand in 1830 gave racing a further boost so that by 1836 Epsom was considered to be of sufficient importance to lead the union of parishes that was set up to administer the Poor Law as described in Chapter Four. 1839 saw the setting up of the Epsom and Ewell Gas Company, 'for the purpose of lighting with gas the towns of Epsom and Ewell', the gasworks being established in East Street. In 1848 the watch house that had stood at the end of the town pond was replaced by the present clock tower.

What really woke up Epsom was the arrival of the railways, the first being the London, Brighton and South Coast Railway Company line from Croydon which opened on 10 May 1847. The line to Brighton opened

25 Epsom High Street showing pond, watchhouse and clock, drawn by John Hassell, 1816, and engraved by H. Summons.

26 St Martin's Church after the rebuilding of 1825 in Commissioners' Gothic style.

27 *Left*. The nave of St Martin's Church, looking west, drawn by Edward Hassell in 1830.

28-9 *Below left*. The present clock tower in the High Street was built in 1848. This design by William Andrews was not accepted. *Below right*. The design that was accepted was by James Butler and Henry Hodge although it was built with a circular, not oval, clock face.

Both designs made provision for the accommodation of the parish fire engine.

30 Epsom acquired its first railway in 1847, provided by the London, Brighton and South Coast Railway Company, with a station in what is now the Upper High Street. This went out of use following the formation of the Southern Railway in 1923, but a station building can still be seen behind the shops.

31 The L.B. & S.C. Railway station in Station Road seen here towards the end of the 19th century.

as early as 1841 on a route that included London Bridge, New Cross, Norwood, Croydon, Redhill, Horley, Three Bridges, Haywards Heath and Brighton. The Croydon-Epsom branch line terminated in an engine shed near the beginning of what is now the Upper High Street, Epsom, with sidings and a station nearby: a station building can still be seen behind

present-day shops and Upper High Street was originally called Station Road.

Law and order became more organised: a court house was built in 1848 in Ashley Road, next to Ashley House, for the County Court, with jurisdiction over all the parishes of the Epsom Union, although the Magistrates continued to meet at *The Albion*.

Public Health

The increasing prosperity did little to improve the living conditions of the poor who were for the most part housed in cramped unsanitary cottages. Conditions were so bad that, following the Public Health Act of 1848, an inquiry into public health in Epsom was held in 1849,

because of the prevalence of typhoid, scarlet fever and a 'low fever' that affected the parish generally. The inquiry revealed that between 1841 and 1848 the life expectancy had gone down from 44 to 40 years.

The report of the inquiry, published on 16 August 1849, refers to Epsom as,

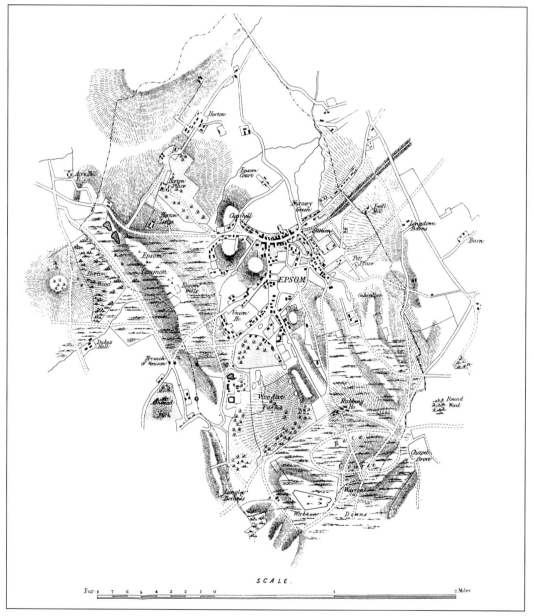

32   The map of Epsom in 1849 that appeared in the report on the public enquiry into the sanitary conditions in Epsom.

a parish and market town with a population upwards of 4,000. There are a tallow chandler and a fellmonger [a dealer in skins or hides] in the town, and two breweries; but besides these, no trades are carried on but such as are necessary to all towns. The poorer classes are almost entirely occupied in the open air: at least one-half in agricultural pursuits, and the other half in the ordinary avocations of labourers in a wealthy country district.

The climate of Epsom is genial. The winds from the Downs and Common are soft and refreshing. Naturally, every circumstance connected with the position of the town is in the highest degree favourable to the health and longevity of the inhabitants. All the medical witnesses concurred in saying that but for its defective sanitary condition it would be exceedingly healthy.

Evidence had been given that the construction of many of the houses in the town was defective, a third of them being built of wood, and so crowded together that there was inadequate ventilation. The privies were mostly wooden cabins close behind the houses discharging into cesspools.

Typical evidence given by a girl living in a cottage in Woodcote Lane was:

My mother has been dead for two years. She went off in a decline. I am 13 years of age, and have two brothers of the ages of 9 and 5 years. My father is a gardener. We have two rooms: one for living and one for sleeping. There is a hole through the wall, and a pigstye and a cowhouse built against the house. There is very often a bad smell in the house. We are obliged to carry all the slops and rubbish to the privy: we have nowhere else to put them. My two little brothers have been sick.

The Inspector expressed concern about the danger of fire as so many of the buildings were of wood: it would spread throughout the town in a very short time and the public fire-engine would be of little use unless the fire was near the pond in the centre of the town.

There was no public water supply and cottagers had to fetch water in pails from the nearest pond or the town pump, which could be half a mile away. Five doctors gave evidence of the effect of the lack of sanitation on the health of the people of Epsom. The town would be a decidedly healthier place if it had good drainage.

The Inspector, William Lee, concluded his comprehensive report by giving detailed proposals on providing a supply of clean water, under pressure, and with a tap and water closet in every house. He thought that, having obtained an abundant supply of water, sewerage and drainage would be easy to accomplish. Earthenware drainage pipes were to be laid throughout the town to convey the whole of the sewerage away to the most suitable locality for its application to the land as liquid manure. William Lee estimated that the water supply could be provided for £3,727 and the drainage for £3,285. The Public Health Act allowed the money to be borrowed on security of the public rates and repaid by annual instalments, with interest, in a period not exceeding 20 years.

Schools

Epsom had a small endowed school before 1800 supported by benefactions left by John Brayne in 1693, David White in 1725 and Elizabeth Northey in 1764. It is likely that a few years after the setting up of the National Society for Promoting the Education of the Poor in the Principles of the Established Church throughout England and Wales in 1811, the charity school in Church Street became a National School. Plans were made for a new National School for 120 boys and 120 girls consisting of two schoolrooms, each 45 feet long and 18 feet wide. It was to be a building of brick with a slate roof, but it was not until 1828 that it was completed. It included a committee room and was built at the East Street end of Hook Road. The school was rebuilt as a mixed school in 1840. By 1844 it became necessary to open a separate infants' school which was provided at West Hill, originally in converted stables.

33 The charity school in Church Street as painted by J. Hassell in 1823, at which date it was probably being used as a National School.

When the Union Workhouse was opened following the setting up of the Epsom Union in 1836 the Managers of the National School allowed 12 boys from the workhouse over eight years of age to attend the school at a charge of £5 a year, the boys to bring their own books. The other children in the Workhouse were to be educated by appointing a schoolmaster and mistress, the former being a pauper inmate who was to be rewarded with 4s. a week and double rations. However, in 1841 the schoolmaster was being paid 12s. a week with lodgings, fire and candles. A report on the Epsom Union School in 1857 when there were 20 boys and 30 girls said that both departments 'passed a very fair exam.'. In 1868 a committee of inspection reported that in the infants' school the 13 infants were washed in one pail with one towel which was changed weekly. More pails and towels were ordered.

With regard to private schools, according to a directory of 1826 several very well conducted academies had been established in Epsom.

Chapter Six

The Second Half of the 19th Century

Following the publication of the report on public health in 1849, in 1850 an Epsom Local Board of Health was elected, but it was not until 1853 that the Water Undertaking was set up. William Lee had proposed obtaining water by draining Epsom Common, but an artesian well in East Street was found to be a better solution. One hundred years later in 1953 all the water needed by Epsom was still being obtained from wells in the vicinity of the original well. Sewers and drains were installed, the sewage being disposed of by an irrigation system on parts of the Epsom Court farmlands after purification. In 1854 the town pond was drained.

Another railway arrived on 4 April 1859 providing a line to Waterloo Station, with the completion of a line from Wimbledon to Epsom which was soon to become part of the London and South Western railway. The station in Epsom was on the site of the present station. A line from Epsom to Leatherhead had been opened on 1 February 1859 and was extended to Dorking and on to Horsham in 1867. The LBSC Railway Company was able to negotiate joint use of the tracks beyond Epsom and a short line was built crossing East Street by a bridge to link the two systems. However, the LBSC Railway Company continued to use its Station Road station until 1929, by which time both companies were part of the Southern Railway.

Victoria Station opened in 1860 after the building of the Grosvenor Bridge to take the railway over the Thames and, with the completion in 1868 of a new line from Peckham Rye to Sutton that included Mitcham Junction, Hackbridge and Carshalton, Epsom had a reasonably direct line to Victoria Station from the Station Road station.

The Epsom Downs station on the branch line from Sutton through Belmont and Banstead opened in 1865 with nine platforms to cater for the race crowds. The Belmont station was originally called California, after a hostelry on the nearby Brighton turnpike road (a local landowner had a connection with the 1849 gold rush). The present Epsom Downs station has only one platform. It was rebuilt farther back down the line than the original station, making space for houses.

Tattenham Corner station on the South Eastern and Chatham Railway opened in 1901. Originally, the service normally terminated at Tadworth, and Tattenham Corner was used only on race days.

The easier access, particularly from London, stimulated trade and also encouraged middle-class commuters to build houses in Epsom. A more direct effect was the arrival of railway workers in the town. The 1851 census shows 16 railway workers, including the station master, engine drivers, guards, engineers, stokers and porters. By 1861 the number of railway workers had increased to about fifty. (The 1861 Census was flawed so one cannot be definite.) The figure for 1891 was fifty-one. (It is interesting that few of them had been born in

SPREAD EAGLE

COMMERCIAL,

FAMILY HOTEL & POSTING HOUSE.

CORNELIUS HUNT, Proprietor.

This well-known Hotel continues to maintain its established reputation for the comfort of its accommodation, the promptness of the attendance, the moderation of the charges, and the excellence of the articles supplied. The proximity to the two Railway Stations, and to the far-famed Downs, afford every facility as well for arrival and departure as for healthy exercise. The Wines and Spirits are genuine, and of the very best quality; and in consequence of the recent Act of Parliament are offered by the Proprietor to the Public on the lowest terms.

The above Hotel contains large, well appointed, cheerful Sitting and Bed Rooms, comfortable Commercial and Coffee Rooms, Billiard and large Assembly Rooms.

A Table d'Hote every Wednesday at half-past 2.

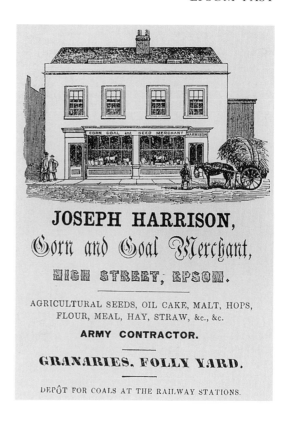

JOSEPH HARRISON,

Corn and Coal Merchant,

HIGH STREET, EPSOM.

AGRICULTURAL SEEDS, OIL CAKE, MALT, HOPS, FLOUR, MEAL, HAY, STRAW, &c., &c.

ARMY CONTRACTOR.

GRANARIES. FOLLY YARD.

DEPÔT FOR COALS AT THE RAILWAY STATIONS.

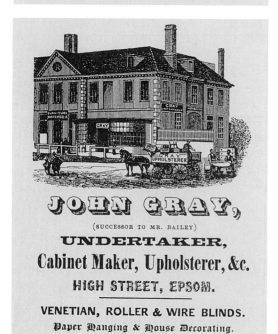

JOHN GRAY,

(SUCCESSOR TO MR. BAILEY)

UNDERTAKER,

Cabinet Maker, Upholsterer, &c.

HIGH STREET, EPSOM.

VENETIAN, ROLLER & WIRE BLINDS.

Paper Hanging & House Decorating.

FURNITURE PACKED, REMOVED & WAREHOUSED

Route Seats kept for Hire.

ESTABLISHED 1798.

34-6 Advertisements published in 1860. John Gray had his premises in Waterloo House.

37 The Epsom (Waterloo) Station built in 1859.

38 The Epsom Downs Station soon after its opening in 1865.

39 *Above*. The Epsom Downs
Station had nine platforms to
cope with the Derby crowds.
The train on the left is the royal
train.

40 *Right*. Epsom High Street,
c.1875.

Epsom: they came from all parts of the country, some as remote as Durham, Lancashire and Yorkshire.)

In 1855 the Home Office approved the erection of a Police Station and it was built at the corner of Ashley Road and Ashley Avenue. In 1864 the Epsom police force had a strength of two sergeants and 11 constables which grew to three sergeants and 19 constables by 1903.

1894 saw the setting up of the Epsom Urban District Council.

The Growth of Population

The population of Epsom of 2,404 in 1801 grew steadily to 3,792 in 1851 after which there was an accelerated growth rate to a figure of 7,721 in 1891. Since full census returns are not available until 100 years after the census, the following comparisons are between 1851 and 1891.

The town grew to accommodate the increased population, the most dramatic increase being in East Street and the surrounding area

which lay in a wedge shape formed by the two railway lines to London, one via Ewell East and the other via Ewell West. Many railway workers lived in this district—there was even a block of cottages known as The Railway Cottages built for their use in what was later called Clayton Road. The district was added to street by street until there were nearly 400 properties whereas the original figure was about one hundred. They were mainly small cottages, some terraced, some semi-detached, although a few villas were built at the Ewell end of the street towards the end of the period.

There was less scope for development in the High Street/Waterloo Road/Ashley Road area, since it was already well populated: however, some 20 additional properties were constructed, and the High Street in 1891 was a mix of shops, craftsmen's establishments and residential properties, with areas of courtyards and alleys filled with cramped accommodation. There were nine inns and public houses, *The Spread Eagle Hotel*, *The King's Head Hotel*, *The Albion*, *The George*, *The Tun*, *The Marquis of Granby*, the *Duke of Wellington*, *The Nag's Head* and *The White Hart*.

The Albion, originally a coffee house, was where magistrates met in Petty Sessions. One outstanding feature of the High Street was the large draper's shop in part of Waterloo House run by John Bailey. The more affluent areas of Epsom such as Woodcote, Church Street and Dorking Road remained affluent areas: the new properties built were substantial houses.

Hamlet of Horton, Pound Lane and Kingston Lane

This totally rural, agricultural area remained a separate entity for the whole 40 years, although a few cottages were built on the lanes leading to it. The number of properties stayed largely unchanged at around thirty. There were two major houses—Horton Place, home of the Trotter family until at least 1881 and Horton Lodge, home of the Willis family for most of the forty years. Henry Willis was a wealthy banker.

John Trotter, the owner of Horton Place in the 1851 Census, had been the Member of Parliament for West Surrey from 1841 to 1847. By 1861 he had been succeeded as owner by his widow Maria and in the 1871 and 1881 Censuses their son William was the owner.

41   Horton Lodge, painted by John Hassell in 1822.

42   The Warren, a house forming part of the hare enclosure on Walton Downs, as photographed in 1914.

The Trotter family were lords of the manor of Horton and both John and William were also magistrates.

There were five major farms that provided employment for many of the agricultural labourers of Epsom. There were no public houses in Horton, which has been referred to as a hamlet of straggling cottages.

The Downs area

In 1851 gypsy families were not recorded, perhaps because they lived in impermanent accommodation, but in 1861 it was stated that seven families were living in caravans, tents or booths on the Downs. The occupations of members of these families were various and included booth-keepers, a basket maker, a mat maker, a cutler and hawkers.

By 1871, 26 families were recorded as living in the area of the Downs, including 11 gypsy households. Some of these gypsies had wonderfully exotic names, such as Spicer, Nelson, Belcha, Merreld, Hezekiah, Orsery and Punch for the men and Geranium, Timminta, Countsalife and Venus for the women. By the following census these names had disappeared and had been replaced by more conventional ones.

At the 1891 Census there was an upsurge of people living in temporary accommodation on the Downs numbering 40 out of the 51 households in the area: all were described as travelling gypsies. In addition another 16 people, largely single men, designated as lodgers, were living in temporary accommodation and were calling themselves mostly labourers and gardeners.

It is probable that there was a race meeting on the Downs at this time, because Mrs. Mary Ann Mitchell at *The Downs Hotel* (the name at the time for *The Rubbing House*) had taken on three female servants 'engaged for race days only'.

Between Epsom and Walton Downs and the Headley Road was Langley Bottom Farm (now Langley Vale Farm). In 1861 Thomas Bowyer farmed 113 acres of land there.

Within the hare warren on Walton Downs was a house known as The Warren, at one time a stud farm. Under the ownership of Benjamin Ellam the house was considerably enlarged to make it suitable for entertaining the distinguished company attracted by racing. It was demolished *c.*1920. North of the Warren were two fields which were to become a large part of the Langley Vale housing estate.

43   A remnant of The Warren seen here in 2000.

Between The Warren and the race course was Downs House, which until 1847, when the position of the course was moved, was within the course. The house with stabling and paddocks had been built by O'Kelly, the owner of Eclipse (see Chapter Eleven) and was in addition to his establishment at Clay Hill. Downs House was originally known as Melision Lodge and during the second half of the 19th century was occupied by the Sherwood family who were trainers, and they had as many as 12 lodgers who would have been jockeys, stable lads and grooms. At that period the house was known as 'Sherwoods'. Downs House is still used by a trainer: the house is not the original but the stables are.

The Economy of Epsom

The table of the approximate numbers of men and women in different work categories taken from census returns illustrates the economy of Epsom during the second half of the 19th century. In 1851 there were more men agricultural workers than men workers in any other category: these workers included farmers, farm bailiffs, market-gardeners, gamekeepers, carters, shepherds, cowmen and agricultural labourers. Of the eight farms, five were in the hamlet of Horton. By 1891 agricultural workers had dropped from 15 per cent to 7 per cent as a percentage of the total work-force of men.

The big houses of the town played an important part in the economy: in 1851 11 per cent of the men (113) were servants, while workers in such categories as building trades, craftsmen, shopkeeepers and gardeners would also have been dependent on the custom of the big houses. There were far more women servants, 308, and this number rose to 638 in 1891, whereas the men rose only to 123 in number.

There was a significant increase in the number of professional men from 57 in 1851 to 263 in 1891. This category included teachers, doctors, dentists, veterinary surgeons, clergymen, lawyers, architects, surveyors, estate agents, clerks, bank managers, stockbrokers, commission agents, merchants and officers in the Army and Navy. There was a corresponding increase in women professionals, nearly all of whom were schoolmistresses.

The growing popularity of racing at Epsom is shown by the increase from 45 to 175 of men employed in racing.

The approximate numbers of men and women in different work categories

MEN

	1851	1891
Agricultural workers	161	152
Labourers	136	336
Building trades	125	195
Craftsmen	126	151
Shopkeepers	113	293
Servants	113	123
Licensed trade	37	43
Public service	57	199
Gardeners	72	98
Racing	45	175
Professionals	57	263
Total	**1,042**	**2,028**

WOMEN

	1851	1891
Servants	308	638
Laundresses	58	152
Craftswomen	39	105
Shopkeepers	39	31
Licensed trade	7	6
Professionals	22	61
Total	**473**	**993**

Some occupations are described in the census returns in an archaic way—there is mention of a beadle, a hosteler (now an ostler), a scavenger (now a road sweeper), letter carriers (postmen), a stay maker and a dry salter (a dealer in chemical products, sauces and pickles). There were also fly-masters, who hired out light one-horse covered carriages, post boys who delivered mail on horseback, a garter maker, a huckster (a stall holder), a blade maker and a strapper (a groom).

Other types of employment that were also a little out of the ordinary included a tea-taster, a crepe dyer, a ginger beer manufacturer, who later turned to making mineral water, a billiard marker, a nutmeg and clove sorter, a bird catcher and a bird-fancier. There was also in 1891 a photographer's male hairdresser who presumably arranged and titivated the hair of those about to be photographed.

Particular careers sound prestigious: John Bladen, aged 77 was Keeper of the Monument, London, in 1861. In 1871 we see recorded John Collier, aged 51, who was Assistant Paymaster-General and John Harding, aged 47 a cathedral organist, while in 1881 and 1891 is featured Colonel James Bullen, Royal Bodyguard. There were other interesting careers in 1891: Charles Batten, professional cricketer, aged 33, Thomas McWatt, professional golfer, aged 27, and Henry Witworth-Mitchell, aged 39, Captain of 11th Hussars (Cavalry).

The occupants of the Workhouse

The composition of the inmates of the Epsom Union Workhouse was more varied than might be thought—some were classed as vagrants, some as paupers, others had their last employment details entered against their names. Many were over 65 years old, but some were younger. A great many were children up to 12 years of age. Some were with their mothers but mostly they were unaccompanied. It must be presumed they were orphans, or abandoned or were there temporarily until their parents' fortunes improved sufficiently to allow them to go back to their homes. In 1851 the Workhouse housed 162 males and 175 females, a total of 337 people, which by 1891 had risen to a total of 415 inmates.

The 1851 Religious Census

The 1851 Census is interesting because in association with it was taken a religious census to determine the number of sittings available in churches and the number of people attending services on 30 March 1851. It was the first and last official religious census.

St Martin's Epsom had 1,100 sittings, only 180 of which were free. The general congregation amounted to 500 in the morning and 230 in the evening. For Christ Church, Epsom Common, no figure was given for the sittings, but it was stated that they were all free. The morning attendance was 100 and 180 in the afternoon.

The Union Chapel (at the Workhouse) had attendances of 200 morning and afternoon. (They would have been a captive congregation.) The non-establishment churches were a Wesleyan Methodist Connexion Chapel, the East Street Chapel (Calvinistic Protestant) and the Church Street Chapel (Congregationalist). The total number of sittings for the non-establishment churches was 556. There was no Roman Catholic church: the few Catholics met in a private house. However, by 1857 St Joseph's Church in Heathcote Road had been built.

The Enclosure of Epsom

As explained in Chapter Two, Epsom had two large common fields to the south of the town that were cultivated by the manorial tenants. There had long been a movement towards the enclosure of such fields, i.e., to divide them into larger, more manageable units. The enclosure of neighbouring Ewell had taken place in 1802 following a specific Act of Parliament. Epsom was not enclosed until 1869, by which time a specific Act of Parliament was no longer required as there had been general Enclosure Acts that set up a standing Enclosure Commission with power to enclose common fields when sufficient local landowners wished it to be done. Actually, by 1869, parts of the Epsom common fields had already been enclosed by private arrangements, particularly at the northern end near the centre of the town, so that the total acreage allotted by the Commissioners was only 535 acres. As was stated in the preamble to the awards, the purpose of the Act was to allow the enclosure, exchange and improvement of land. The Enclosure map shows nearly 200 strips in the fields. Allotments were made to more than 50 recipients in proportion to their respective rights and interest in the land. The biggest allotment was to the heirs of the late Alexander Wood, who received about 120 acres, whereas several received less than a quarter of an acre.

In the case of Ewell, enclosure led to the formation of large farms, whereas the Epsom allotments were mostly developed for housing.

Hospitals

Epsom's first Cottage Hospital opened in 1873 at Pembroke Cottages, Pikes Hill, but was moved to Hawthorne Place in 1877. The town decided that a new hospital would be a good way to commemorate the Golden Jubilee of Queen Victoria so one was erected on a new site in Alexandra Road and was opened by Princess Mary, Duchess of Teck, in 1889. It was a voluntary hospital supported by donations until it became part of the newly formed National Health Service in 1948. In fact the Cottage Hospital continued to benefit from voluntary support that enabled it to provide facilities that would not otherwise have been possible. It kept strong links with local general practitioners who could assist consultants in the main operating theatre, and have facilities to carry out minor operations themselves in the out-patients' theatre. However, in 1988 the Cottage Hospital was transferred to new premises in the grounds of West Park Hospital and the Alexandra Road hospital was taken over by a large group practice of doctors. Since 1994, part has been run as a day case surgical unit.

What is now Epsom District Hospital was opened in 1890 under the Poor Law Guardians, which explains why it was built adjacent to the Union Workhouse. In addition to the general hospital, an isolation hospital for infectious diseases was built in Hook Road, where Tomlin Court is now.

44   The Cottage Hospital in 1910. It was built to commemorate the Golden Jubilee of Queen Victoria.

Social Life

The growing affluence of Epsom towards the end of the century is signalled by the many clubs and similar organisations that were established. The Epsom Branch of the Ancient Order of Foresters came into being *c.*1860 and flourished until towards the end of the 20th century. Lord Rosebery was initiated as a Forester in 1899. A golf club was formed in 1889 and a cycling club in 1891. (A cricket club had been formed much earlier, some time prior to 1800, in fact. In the early days it had played on the Downs, acquiring its present ground in Woodcote Road around 1860.)

A Public Hall was built in 1883 at the corner of Station Road and Church Street facing the High Street. It was of red brick and terracotta, the architect being a local man, J. Hatchard Smith, who was later responsible for the Technical Institute that was built alongside the Public Hall. The hall was the venue for meetings, lectures and concerts, and was run by the Epsom Public Hall and Assembly Rooms Co. Ltd.

Lord Rosebery was a leading patron of the Epsom Choral Society and the Epsom Orchestral Society which gave their first joint concert in 1897 in the Epsom Public Hall with 77 voices in the choir and a 41-piece orchestra.

In 1898 what is now known as Epsom, Ewell and District Literary Society was inaugurated, replacing the Epsom and Ewell Literary and Scientific Institution that had been founded some fifty years earlier but had to close due to financial problems and lack of members. The Institution had premises in the High Street.

45 Cyclists outside *The Rising Sun, c.*1890.

46 In 1878 Epsom welcomed Lord Rosebery and his new bride.

EPSOM AND EWELL
LITERARY AND SCIENTIFIC INSTITUTION.

The Fifth of a Second Series of

READINGS

WILL BE GIVEN

On WEDNESDAY, 10th DECEMBER, 1862,

IN THE LECTURE ROOM OF THE INSTITUTION.

SUBJECT	AUTHOR	READER.
Rural Life in England ..	Irving	Mr. J. Harrowell, Jun.
Rather hard to take	Anon	Mr. F. Marfleet.
The Broken Crutch	Bloomfield ..	Rev. J. Donovan, B.A.
The One Legged Goose .	Anon	Mr. J. Andrews.
Story of Le Fevre	Sterne	Mr. Murrell.
Doings at Do the Boys Hall	Dickens ..	Mr. S. Marfleet.

Doors open at ½ to 8 o'Clock, Reading to commence at ¼ past 8 PRECISELY.
Admission :—THREEPENCE.   Members FREE.

Gentlemen willing to assist in the Readings will much OBLIGE by forwarding
their Names and Subjects (which should not occupy more than ten to fifteen
minutes in the reading) to the Secretary at their earliest convenience.

☞ THESE READINGS ARE GIVEN EVERY ALTERNATE WEDNESDAY.

Andrews, Printer, High Street, Epsom.

47   The programme for a meeting of the Epsom and Ewell Library and Scientific Institution.

48   The Station Road and Church Street junction, *c.*1900, with the public hall built in 1883 on the right.

49 Epsom College, *c*.1896. It had been founded in 1853 to help retired medical men and widows as well as providing education for doctors' sons.

50 The 1896 building erected as the Epsom Technical Institute with some fine terracotta ornamentation.

Schools in the second half of the 19th century

The growing population made bigger schools necessary. The Hook Road School had to be enlarged in 1886 and again in 1896. The girls had been transferred to a new school built in Ladbroke Road in 1871, and that also had to be enlarged. The West Hill Infants School was enlarged in 1872 and a new infants school built at Hawthorne Place in 1893. Under an arrangement made in 1887 the schools came under a committee of managers consisting of eight trustees of Brayne's charity and eight others who were elected annually, reporting to the District Council.

1853 saw the foundation of The Royal Medical Benevolent College by John Propert, a Welsh surgeon, on land given by Dr. Graham, who lived at Woodcote End. It was intended to help retired medical men and widows in financial straits as well as providing education for doctors' sons. By 1861 there were 128 pupils aged 10-17 and in addition 16 elderly people, mostly widows of doctors, sometimes alone but mostly accompanied in their apartment by a servant or close relative. By 1891 there were about 200 boarding pupils, 11 school teachers and 40 college servants. The number of pensioners had dropped to 13, with eight staff.

Young ladies were catered for by a High School for Young Ladies in Church Street and a Ladies' College at Downside.

1896 saw the opening by Lord Rosebery of the Epsom Technical Institute in a fine terracotta ornamented building in Church Street built by public subscription, prominent subscribers being Major Coates of Tayles Hill and Basil Braithwaite of Hookfield. It was later taken over by Surrey County Council.

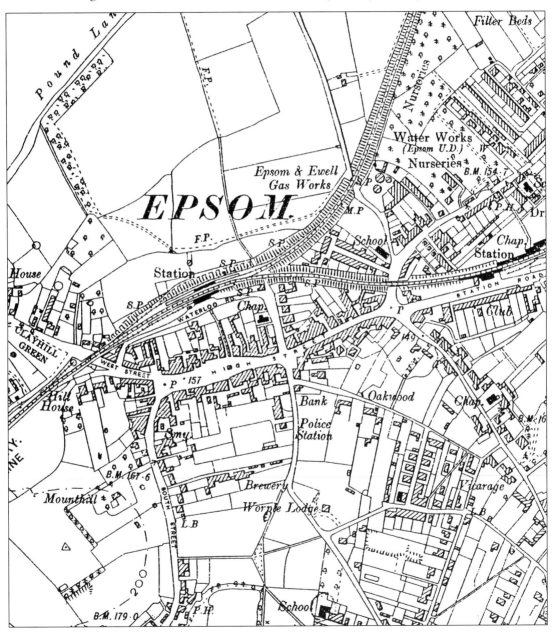

51 Epsom on the Ordnance Survey map, surveyed 1866-7, revised in 1894-5, published in 1897.

Chapter Seven

Epsom Common

Epsom Common is a large area of land (approximately 500 acres), roughly triangular in shape, to the west of the town. In 1794 it was described as 'being covered with furze, brambles, hawthorn bushes, large quantities of hornbeams and other pollards: other parts are sour, wet pasture'. The heavy clay soil is unsuitable for cultivation.

The Common was the property of the lord of the manor, but local people had long established, jealously guarded rights on the common which, in addition to free access, included rights of pasture and the gathering of turves or gorse for fuel. Bracken could be collected for thatch and cattle bedding, and wood for fires, but not timber from trees.

There was early settlement around the edges of the Common, particularly at Stamford Green: a survey of 1679 indicated a mill by the pond, the miller's house, a tile kiln as well as cottages and a village green.

52 Stamford Green with its pond was an early place of settlement on the Common.

By 1755 there had been a considerable amount of squatter development on the Common with more than 30 cottages, and the steward of the manor had to record that they were held 'by what rent or service we know not'. The majority of them lay on the land between Stamford Green and the well. In his 1849 report, William Lee had commented:

'There is a considerable number of cottages on the Common, said to have been erected on the waste, and the owners to have ultimately acquired freeholds by lapse of time. They form quite a colony distinct from the town.' The problems arising from the lack of piped water and drains were as bad as anywhere in Epsom.

By the beginning of the 19th century so many cottages had been erected on the Common that it became necessary to consider building a chapel of ease to encourage church attendance as it was more than a mile to St Martin's Church. The Rev. Benjamin Bockett obtained the Bishop's permission, and he was able to raise the necessary funds from subscriptions from church building societies, parishioners and friends. A piece of land was given by Mr. J.I. Briscoe, the lord of the manor, and a small church seating fewer than 200 persons was built in red brick on the site of the scout headquarters that is to the left of the present Christ Church. It was consecrated in July 1845.

The population on the Common soon outgrew the little church and in her will Miss Elizabeth Trotter of Horton Manor left £8,000 to cover the building of a bigger church, its endowment and the provision of a parsonage, with the proviso that a new parish should be created. Another condition was that there should be 'no ritualistic nonsense'. The new parish of Christ Church was created by an Order in Council in July 1874 and work on the new church went ahead to the designs of a well-known Gothic Revival architect, Sir Arthur Blomfield. It was consecrated by the Bishop of Winchester in October 1876. The

53 The haphazard development of parts of the common has resulted in an interesting variety of buildings, including one known as The Castle.

£8,000 bequeathed by Miss Trotter was insufficient to pay for the work and more funds had to be raised by a public appeal. Other members of the Trotter family contributed £2,000 and various church authorities and charities made contributions to enable the total expenditure of £15,000 to be met. The old church was demolished in 1877.

Lord Rosebery worshipped at Christ Church and he paid for a south aisle to be added, work that was completed in 1879. The east window was in memory of Elizabeth Trotter who had died in 1868: unfortunately bombing in 1941 damaged the window beyond repair and a new one was put in in 1952 by James Powell and Sons. Another memorial to Elizabeth Trotter is the stone font given by Mr. E. Northey.

The tower was not completed in the initial building: it was necessary to raise more money for its completion in 1887. An outstanding feature of Christ Church is the rood-screen in wrought iron and bronze with richly ornamented traceried panels that was installed

54 Christ Church was consecrated in 1876 and was intended to serve people living on the Common.

55 Christ Church was designed by the well known Gothic Revival architect, Sir Arthur Blomfield.

56 The screen in wrought iron and bronze, richly ornamented, was to the design of C.H. Fellowes Prynne and was dedicated to the memory of William Sampson Trotter in 1909.

57 In Christ Church there is a memorial window to Lt. Col. Francis Northey, who died in action in Zululand in 1879.

in 1909 to the design of C.H. Fellowes Prynne. It was erected in memory of William Sampson Trotter by his wife, son and daughter.

The cottagers developed into a close-knit community. In 1663 a licence had been granted to dig clay and make bricks and tiles on the Common and the brick works by Wheelers Lane near *The Jolly Coopers* was in operation for more than 200 years, providing employment for local people. Many of the large houses put up in the spa period were built from bricks made on the Common.

Another source of employment on the Common was the windmill that was situated to the north east of the mineral water well within the circle that had been cleared around it (see Chapter Three). The earliest documentary reference to the mill is in 1795. It was sold by auction in 1809 and the sale notice reveals that it was a post mill 14 feet wide with two pairs of stones; the sails carried 11 yards of canvas. The sale included various implements and utensils as well as two draught horses, a van, a cart and two pigs. Other references to the mill indicate that it was one of the largest post mills in England, with a sail span of 72 feet. The mill came to a spectacular end in about 1880 when it caught fire and burnt down with its sails revolving like a giant Catherine wheel.

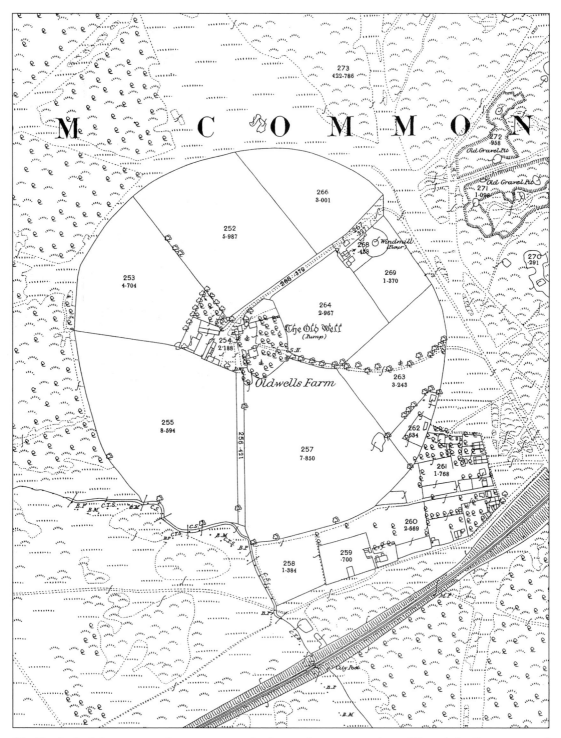

58 The lord of the manor took away common land status from an area about 450 yards in diameter around the well. This shows it in 1867 when it contained Oldwells Farm. The shape can be recognised in the present housing estate.

The area around the well remained largely undeveloped until recent times. The old well house was pulled down in 1804 and farm buildings of Oldwells Farm were erected; these were demolished when the lord of the manor, James Stuart Strange, had a mansion erected in 1885.

When in 1899 the Mental Hospitals arrived in Epsom with the opening of Horton Manor Asylum, it was against the wishes of most Epsom residents. However, the hospitals needed a wide range of workers, male and female; cooks, laundresses, needlewomen, joiners, plumbers and many others—even agricultural workers were required, for the farms and gardens associated with the hospitals. People living on the Common benefited: they were able to get employment at the hospitals, at higher wages and with less travelling than previously.

Something that helped mould the residents into a community was the founding in 1880 of the Working Men's Club at the initiative and expense of Mr. Strange, the lord of the manor. The building erected for the club was described as 'handsome and commodious' and was later bought by the members. As well as providing a meeting place where people could have refreshments, the club sponsored a wide range of activities: cricket matches, outings and all sorts of celebrations.

An outstanding feature of the Common is the Great Pond adjacent to the Stew Pond that was created in medieval times probably by monks of Chertsey Abbey by building a dam, but on the evidence of maps it was drained by breaching the dam sometime between 1843 and 1867. However, in 1975 work began on rebuilding the dam so that the pond could be refilled, work that was organised by the Epsom

59 The well-head that was built over the well in 1989.

Common Association, using largely voluntary labour. The project led to a commendation by the Civic Trust in 1980. The recreated pond has an area of about nine acres.

In 1936 the Common was bought by Epsom and Ewell Urban District Council from Henrietta Langley Strange, the lady of the manor, for £4,000, so that since then the rights of the Common have been vested in the Council as a corporate body, and the Common is maintained by the Parks Department.

Chapter Eight

The 20th Century until 1939

The railways, improvements in public health, racing, and its position as a shopping centre for the surrounding area, in which there were many big houses, brought prosperity to Epsom and by the beginning of the 20th century it was a well-organised, self-reliant community with a confident Urban District Council under its Chairman Henry Mayson Dorling, J.P. One of the eight other members was Lord Rosebery. In addition to the Clerk to the Council, the officials included a Surveyor and Inspector of Nuisances, an Engineer and an Overseer and Collector of the Poor Rate. The council met fortnightly at Bromley Hurst, a large house in Church Street. It acted also as the Burial Board and School Attendance Committee.

60 Crowds outside the polling station for the 1906 election when W. Keswick was elected Member of Parliament.

61   Epsom High Street, *c.*1910.

Clubs abounded: in addition to Conservative, Liberal and Working Men's Clubs there was the non-political Epsom Club that met in the Public Hall. Other associations included the Foresters, the Independent Order of Oddfellows, the Surrey Agricultural Society and angling, horticultural, orchestral and choral societies. There was a golf club and the Epsom and Ewell Fanciers Association. There were four Epsom newspapers in 1903: the *Journal*, the *Herald*, the *Observer* and the *Epsom and District Times*.

The town was protected by the Fire Brigade operating from its station in Waterloo Road to which the firemen were summoned by electric bells. The streets were well lit by gas supplied by the Epsom and Ewell Gas Company. By 1902 electricity became available from the Council's generating station in Depot Road.

The Rev. W. Bainbridge Bell, who became vicar in 1904, considered that St Martin's was too small for his large parish, a view shared by the Earl of Rosebery and

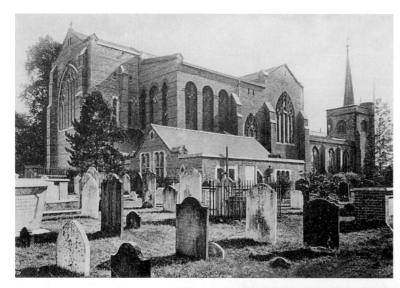

62 The rebuilding work on St Martin's parish church, completed in 1908, gave a chancel and transepts of cathedral-like proportions.

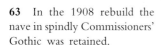

63 In the 1908 rebuild the nave in spindly Commissioners' Gothic was retained.

ambitious plans were made for enlargement to almost cathedral-like proportions. Subscriptions were raised and work began by building a new east end with crossing and transepts in place of the old chancel, work that was completed in 1908. The new nave and tower envisaged were never built, leaving what has been described as an oddly composite building. The west front and the nave with its aisles are of spindly Commissioners' Gothic, with thin perpendicular piers, whereas the rebuilt east end is a massive construction of dark brown stone with some flint work, of an indeterminate Gothic style.

The new east end was built on a different alignment to the old nave, so one is aware that the chancel is askew in relation to the nave. The shingled spire on the old tower was taken down in 1947 following storm damage.

In 1909 another church was consecrated, St Barnabas, a large red-brick building in Temple Road, north of the town centre. It replaced a temporary corrugated iron mission church that had been erected to serve the growing population of the staff of the large mental hospitals that were being built. In 1919 St Barnabas was given its own parish, rather

64   The west end of St Martin's was unaffected by the rebuild. The shingled spire that can be seen in this picture was taken down in 1947 following storm damage.

65   This model of St Martin's, made by a parishioner, makes clear the contrast between the 1825 west end and the 1908 east end.

66 Shops in Pound Lane, an area that was developed in the early 20th century to house the staff of the mental hospitals.

67 The Electrical Theatre Cinema became the Pavilion Theatre, but closed in 1929, although it was not demolished until 1953.

than being a daughter church of Christ Church.

The first cinema arrived in 1910, the Electrical Theatre Cinema, built at the junction of East Street and Hook Road. It became the Pavilion Theatre in 1926, but in 1929 it closed, although the building was not demolished until 1953. The Electrical Theatre was shortly followed by the Cinema Royal at the junction of Church Street and High Street on the south side. Sound was installed in 1929 and it was able to stay open until 1938.

1910 also saw the setting up by public subscription of Epsom Town Dispensary to bring advice and treatment to the poorest inhabitants on medical matters, midwifery and dentistry. The dental work covered extractions only, 6d. per tooth without anaesthetic or 2s. 6d. with.

Study of the minutes of the Urban District Council for 1911 gives a good idea of the concerns at that time. It was agreed that the cost of a loyal address to be presented to King George V on the occasion of his coronation should not exceed £5. Surrey County Council were to be asked to give urgent attention to fixing a speed limit through Epsom. Gas lighting had been replaced by electric lighting, and a recommendation that extensions to the power station should use diesel engines rather than steam engines was approved. Consideration was also given to a proposal for the amalgamation of the Gas Company with those of Wandsworth and Wimbledon.

The installation of an inter-communication system of telephones between Council departments was vetoed by the Finance Committee: the Accountant's Office and Sanitary Inspector's Office were to use the telephone in the Surveyor's Department. The report by the Inspector of Cows on the condition of the 90 milk cows in the Urban District was approved.

There was a noteworthy event on 18 May 1912 when the UK's first public automatic telephone exchange was opened at Epsom. The equipment was installed in the Post Office exchange in Station Road by the Automatic Electric Company of Chicago and had provision for 500 lines. It replaced a manual exchange that had been put in in 1905. There were several reasons why Epsom was chosen for this first public experiment: these included the high

percentage of local traffic and its situation in the system in relation to the London Central Exchange and other call centres. Furthermore, it was considered that the high rate of calls on race days would be a good test for the automatic switches. An unexpected increase in calls arose a few years later when Epsom became a dispersal point for war hospitals.

The First World War

The response to the outbreak of war on 3 August 1914 was patriotic fervour: men clamoured to join up and two days later 60 local Territorials marched to the railway station to entrain for Chatham. A recruiting meeting on 28 August attracted a large crowd that was addressed by Mr. Basil Braithwaite, a leading magistrate: 'God Save the King' was sung and 27 men enlisted. More did so on subsequent days, so that the body of recruits that boarded the motor cars that had been hired to take them to Kingston on 1 September was sizeable. Mr. Braithwaite was there to see them off, and to exhort them to 'Do your duty bravely, fear God and honour the King'. (Basil Braithwaite lived at Hookfield House, a large

68 Sydney Martin, a horse-drawn ambulance driver, won the Medaille Militaire in France in September 1914 for rescuing wounded men under fire. He is seen here with his wife, Matilda, and sons Sidney and Walter.

69 The University and Public Schools Brigade of the Royal Fusiliers built a camp for themselves in Woodcote Park.

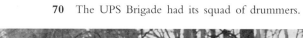

70 The UPS Brigade had its squad of drummers.

71   The UPS Brigade marching past Waterloo House in 1914.

mansion at West Hill, now demolished. He was Chairman of the local Recruiting Committee.) The following day another 35 recruits were given a similar send-off. The enthusiasm to become involved was such that, when a force of special constables was set up, by mid-September it numbered 200. Their role was to police danger spots where the enemy might attack.

At the same time as men were leaving Epsom, there was an influx of recruits into the town, men who had joined the University and Public Schools Brigade of the Royal Fusiliers which was planned to consist of four battalions and have a total strength of 5,000 men. It was an unusual brigade in that it was raised by a civilian committee chaired by Sir Arthur Stanley who was also Chairman of the Royal Automobile Club, which in 1913 had purchased Woodcote Park, Epsom, and this was where the UPS Brigade was to be stationed: the site

had been commandeered by the War Office. It took time to build the necessary accommodation for these new soldiers, and so initially they were billeted in homes throughout Epsom, Ashtead, Headley and Leatherhead. They spent their days constructing a huge hutted camp in Woodcote Park for their own use. It was not until March 1915 that the four UPS battalions were able to move into their quarters and by the following month 3,000 men were quartered there. It was a brief occupation, because in May 1915 the brigade was moved to Clipstowe in Nottinghamshire. It later went to France where it took part in trench warfare and was virtually wiped out in the battle of Delville Wood in 1916, after which three of the four battalions were disbanded, the men who had survived being transferred to other battalions or cadet schools. When the UPS moved out, the Woodcote camp became the Woodcote Convalescent Camp.

72 20,000 troops were lined up on The Downs on 22 January 1915 to await inspection by Lord Kitchener.

The brigade had a considerable impact during its few months in Epsom: landladies received 24s. a week for each man billeted with them, a considerable sum of money in 1914 which brought an unaccustomed prosperity to some parts of the town. Before leaving, the troops organised an informal parade to show their appreciation to the townspeople for their cordial welcome and their spokesman made a special reference to the hospitality of the landladies.

Epsom had acquired its first military hospital immediately after war broke out, when the recently-built service block behind the grandstand was taken over and converted to a hospital. The Grand Stand Hospital became an auxiliary to the war hospital that Horton Asylum was converted into in March 1915. A portion of land in the Ashley Road Cemetery was set aside for men who died in the war hospitals. The first one buried there on 17 July 1915 was given a full military funeral.

Before its departure the UPS Brigade took part in a parade of 20,000 troops on The Downs that included also the 2nd London Division of Lord Kitchener's New Army, men from the London Scottish Regiment stationed at Dorking and the London Reserve Infantry

Brigade from Horley and Reigate. The date was 22 January 1915: it had been snowing, and was so bitterly cold that a number of men were overcome and had to be taken to the Grand Stand Hospital. The troops were inspected by Lord Kitchener, Secretary of State for War, accompanied by the French Minister of War, M. Millerand. These dignataries arrived by motor car shortly after 10.30 a.m. and left their vehicle to inspect the troops on foot, but they could not have seen many of the 20,000 assembled men as they did not remain for more than five minutes.

Having so many soldiers in the town made more work for the police and there were numerous summonses, the most common offence being for having over-bright headlamps on cars, motorcycles and bicycles. It had been decreed that lights should be dimmed in towns in anticipation of air raids.

Civilians rallied round to help the war effort: Miss Nora Willis and Miss F.Hamilton Pott enlisted as part-time voluntary 'postmen' to relieve men joining the forces. They were the first lady 'postmen' in the country.

By the beginning of 1916 men aged between 18 and 40 no longer had a choice about serving in the forces, since they were conscripted by the Military Service Act of 27 January that year. A tribunal was set up at Bromley Hurst to consider applications for exemption, but where an application was accepted it was usually for a few months only. Alfred Randall, mineral water manufacturer, claimed exemption on the grounds that he was the only one in the business who understood the manufacturing side. Mr. A. Elphick, a butcher, wished to retain the services of Thomas Choule, 'as he was the only one on the premises beside the applicant who could kill a bullock'. Exemption was granted until 1 July.

It was in 1916 that an Australian trooper recuperating after action at Gallipoli was fined for assaulting a police officer when he had taken exception to being disturbed while in the churchyard with his girlfriend. A fellow trooper had become involved and he too ended up in court. The two troopers were fined £10 and £5 with costs respectively.

Not unrelated to the military presence was the fine of an Epsom woman for permitting her house to be used for immoral purposes. On the other side of the coin was news about the re-opening in Ashley Road of St Monica's Home for Preventative and Rescue Work, 'for those who wished to save themselves from themselves'.

On 6 July 1916 Lord Rosebery went to Woodcote Park Convalescent Camp to open a tea-room. It turned into a solemn occasion, because in his speech he had to announce the death of Lord Kitchener, lost on the cruiser *Hampshire* when it struck a mine off the Orkneys on the way to Russia. On 18 July 1916 King George V and Queen Mary visited Woodcote Park after lunch with Lord Rosebery at Durdans and later went to the Horton war hospital.

By 1917 the war that was to have been over by Christmas 1914 was still going on and was biting even harder. There were shortages of food, particularly sugar, flour and meat, and prices went up. Although public houses continued to open, the hours were restricted and the price of a bottle of whisky went up

from 4s. to 5s. 6d. Beer went up from 4½d. to 6½d. a bottle.

The casualty lists grew longer: few families escaped the dreaded telegram telling them that a husband, father or son had been killed in action or was missing. Lord Rosebery's favourite son, Neil, was killed near Gaza, a blow from which Rosebery never recovered. Raymond Norrington, son of Edward Norrington, family butcher, was killed in action in August 1917. He had worked as a clerk at the London County and Westminster Bank Ltd in High Street, Epsom, before joining up as a private. Trefelyn Roland Cropley, son of Charles Cropley, died in December 1917 as a sergeant in the Queen's Westminster Rifles. Cropley, a builder, was Chairman of the Urban District Council. When Basil Braithwaite opened the New Year sessions of the Magistrates Court in 1918, he said that he was unable to offer the conventional greetings while what the Prime

73 Raymond, son of Epsom butcher, Edward Norrington, photographed with his father on 3 July 1917. A month later he was killed in action.

74   Epsom Police Station after the riot by Canadian soldiers in June 1919.

Minister had described as 'an unspeakable agony of nations' was going on.

Waldegrave Bainbridge Bell, who had initiated the rebuilding of the parish church before the war, returned from service as a padre and resumed his duties as vicar. It was noted that he put into practice observations made in France so that his services were brighter and shorter than before.

In October 1918 the town was struck by the influenza epidemic that was raging throughout the world causing schools, shops and businesses to be closed. In March the age for conscription had been raised to 50 and it was necessary to grant a grave digger three months' exemption to cope with the deaths arising from the epidemic.

The end of the war on 11 November 1918 brought scenes of public revelry and rejoicing: the entire population took to the streets. There were impromptu parades by schoolboys and soldiers to the sound of whistles and tin drums; flags flew and bonfires blazed. Business was suspended in most establishments and churches held services to offer thanks for the end of four years of misery.

Armistice Day did not see the immediate withdrawal of troops from Epsom: Canadian soldiers were still there in June 1919. They were in a restive mood and, when one of their members was locked up in the Police Station for disorderly behaviour, some of his mates stormed the building and in the melée Station Sergeant Thomas Green was killed in its defence.

Epsom commemorated its dead with a war memorial that was unveiled on Sunday 11 December 1921 in front of a great crowd. It took the form of a Celtic cross 18 feet high standing on a three-tier base, all in granite, and situated at the northern end of the Ashley Road

75 The memorial to Station Sergeant Thomas Green, who was killed during the riot by Canadian troops in June 1919.

76 The 256 Epsom people who were killed in the First World War are commemorated by the memorial at the northern end of Ashley Road Cemetery, seen here in 1924.

77 There is a separate memorial for the service people who died in the Epsom war hospitals.

Cemetery. James Chuter Ede as Chairman accepted responsibility on behalf of the Urban District Council. The memorial was completed two years later by the addition of flanking walls and panels bearing the names of the 256 Epsom people who had been killed in the war.

Development of Epsom

The arrival of the railways in 1847 and 1859 boosted the population of Epsom, and it was given another boost following the formation of the Southern Railway in 1923 which absorbed the two companies that served Epsom. More particularly, it was the electrification of the lines that made the difference, that to Waterloo in 1925 and that to Victoria in 1929. Epsom Town Station in what is now Upper High Street, on the line to Victoria, was closed, and Epsom Station was rebuilt and extended to serve both lines. The Southern Railway did

all that it could to attract developers and commuters to the areas served by its network.

From 1928 onwards development started to the north of the station with shops and houses along Waterloo Road and houses in Chase Road. There followed estates along Copse Edge Avenue, near Epsom College, Horsley Close, The Chase and Hookfield Road.

There was development around other stations in the area also: Epsom Downs had Ruden Way and Drift Bridge. The annual number of passengers using the station rose from 330,000 in 1927 to 850,000 in 1935. The Surrey Downs Estate by Tattenham Corner was advertised as 'set amid the fairy lands of Surrey, 600 feet above sea-level on dry chalky soil swept by sweet air direct from the Southern Seas'.

A new cinema, the Capitol, opened in 1929 at the High Street end of Church Street. The name was changed to The Granada Cinema in 1947 and it remained open until 1960. For the period 1930-36 it put on stage shows on Sunday evenings.

In 1930 Epsom Hospital became the responsibility of the Health Committee of the Surrey County Council. Associated legislation aimed at the break-up of the Poor Law led to the Board of Guardians of the Workhouse having its last meeting in 1930.

Epsom High Street received a new look in the 1930s when the eastern end down to Waterloo Road was widened by demolishing the buildings on the north side. Not everyone was in favour of this, and a public inquiry had to be held before the scheme could go ahead. This was directed by the Minister of Transport to see whether confirmation could be given to the compulsory purchase of lands 'for the purpose of widening, opening, enlarging or otherwise improving the streets known as Waterloo Road and High Street'. The inquiry took place at Myers Hall, Ashley Road, Epsom,

78   E. Turner set up his bakery business at 92, East Street, *c.*1920. It prospered and in the 1930s branches were set up in Ewell, Cheam and Sutton. The firm remained in business until long after the end of the Second World War.

79 Skinner's dairy started in East Street *c.*1900 and was in business until *c.*1920 with premises also in Pound Lane.

80 The Southern Railway rebuilt Epsom Station in Art Deco style.

81   When Epsom High Street was widened in the mid-1930s some of the old buildings were not demolished until after the new ones had been put up.

on 21 July 1933. In 1934 The Public Hall was demolished, allowing the construction of The Quadrant parade of shops. Also in 1934 was the building of the Magistrates Court in Ashley Road.

When the Epsom Urban District Council was created in 1894, an Epsom Rural District Council had also been set up and had taken over the responsibilities of the Epsom Rural Sanitary Authority. Local government was re-organised in 1933 by the Surrey Review Order and the Epsom Rural District Council was abolished, its responsibilities being shared among neighbouring authorities. The old parish of Ewell, most of Cuddington and bits of other parishes were transferred to the Epsom Urban District Council, the name of which was changed to Epsom and Ewell Urban District

Council. The enlarged authority applied for its status to be raised to that of a borough with its own corporation, and it received its charter on 29 September 1937, with appropriate pomp and ceremony. The combined population of Epsom and Ewell in 1931 before the amalgamation was around 35,000 and the population of the Borough in 1991 was around 66,000. One of the first buildings opened by the new borough was the Public Baths in 1938, with a swimming pool, slipper baths and a Turkish bath.

1937 had seen the opening of the Odeon Cinema in the High Street, almost opposite Waterloo House. It was considered at the time to be the last word in cinema construction and it survived until 1971. In 1938 a new County Court was built in The Parade, replacing the old building in Ashley Road.

82 The Borough of Epsom and Ewell received its charter on 29 September 1937 in a ceremony in front of the clock-tower.

83   May Day at Pound Lane School, 1912.

Schools

The situation regarding schools at the end of the 19th century is set out in Chapter Six. A detailed account of the many changes that occurred in subsequent years is beyond the scope of this book. However, a few of the most important developments will be sketched in.

1907 saw the building by Surrey County Council of a large school in Pound Lane for 600 boys and girls and 185 infants, enabling some of the smaller schools to be closed. The Pound Lane School had a large hall that came into its own on May Days. The hall was decked with flowers and greenery: a May Queen paraded, attended by maids in white dresses and pageboys in pea-green, watched by an audience of parents, local gentry and members of Surrey County Council. A tradition was established that continued up to the start of the Second World War. The Epsom Central School, a junior technical college, was opened in 1937 in Danetree Road.

In 1921 part of the old Technical Institute became the Epsom County Secondary School for girls, but six years later they moved to purpose-built accommodation in White Horse Drive named after Lord Rosebery. The building they left became the Epsom County School for boys. The County Council obtained a playing field for their use at Hessle Grove, and later this became the site of a new building for the County School for boys that opened in September 1938. Langley Vale acquired a school in 1923 in what was regarded as a temporary structure, but which in fact remained in use until something bigger and better was built in 1998.

An important addition to the Independent Schools was the opening in 1928 of the Convent of the Sacred Hearts School in Dorking Road. The grounds of the convent were big enough to accommodate a farm with miscellaneous animals as well as an orchard and vegetable garden. The school closed c.1990.

Chapter Nine

The Second World War and After

The Second World War

The outbreak of war on 3 September 1939 did not find Epsom and Ewell unprepared since, in the early 1930s, local authorities had been required by central government to organise and part-finance air-raid precautions within their own areas. Air-raid wardens and associated workers were recruited and trained. In the borough a network of wardens' posts was set up and at the beginning of the war there were about 140 full-time paid wardens and some 560 volunteer wardens and messengers. They worked in teams of eight or so from wardens' posts each intended to serve about 500 inhabitants, a total of 55 posts in the borough.

Air-raid shelters

Early in 1939 the builders M.J. Gleesons were contracted by the Borough Council to construct six large public air-raid shelters made from pre-cast concrete panels below ground level and covered with about two feet of soil. The ones in Epsom were at Rosebery Park (1,440 persons) and Clay Hill Green (180 persons). Some householders built their own shelters in their cellars, garages or gardens: others had the officially issued Anderson shelters.

Later in the war two large underground shelters were made in Epsom, one on Epsom Downs opposite the old railway station, and another in Ashley Road on the opposite side

84   The Ashley Road air-raid shelter was tunnelled into the chalk some 30 feet below the surface and was brick lined.

of the road to the cemetery and to the north of it. These shelters were tunnelled into the chalk some 30 feet below the surface and each was provided with 1,500 bunk beds and toilet, canteen and first-aid facilities. Some public brick-built surface shelters were also constructed, and schools, hospitals and factories had to have shelters built.

In September 1941 after prolonged bombing the Morrison shelter was introduced for people who could no longer exist in damp and badly ventilated Anderson shelters. The Morrison shelter was a heavy steel table under which people could shelter in their own homes, on the ground floor, in the hope that, if the house was bombed, they would survive in the ruins until a rescue team could dig them out.

The war effort

The war effort was not confined to the thousands of young men and women who joined the armed forces and left the borough: all those left behind played their part. Home food production was of vital importance and 'dig for victory' became the slogan. Any suitable areas of land were used as allotments, something like 2,300 of them in the borough.

The farms were worked to full capacity and additional areas of land were put under the plough. Land girls, members of the Women's Land Army, became a familiar sight in and around Epsom. Organisation of the Women's Land Army began some three months before the start of the war. Initially, farmers doubted the ability of the girls to work as well as men, but they soon proved their worth. A recruitment booklet stated:

> There is a place in the Land Army today for every young woman who is fit and strong, who cares for country things and prefers hard work and long hours in the open air to hard work and long hours in the factory ... The Land Army fights in the fields. It is in the fields of Britain that the most critical battle of the present war may well be fought and won.

The booklet gave lots of practical advice for the Land Girl, including the following:

> A certain amount of make-up may be used at parties and local village dances, but long nails are quite unsuited to work on a farm, especially when covered with bright crimson nail varnish. She will find too, that she will get such a healthy colour to her cheeks that rouging will not be necessary!

The Women's Land Army was 100 per cent women, from top to bottom, and very much in the control of 'county' ladies. Each county had its Chairman and the list could have come out of Debrett, with many titled ladies, including, for Derbyshire, Her Grace the Duchess of Devonshire and, for Northamptonshire, The Countess Spencer. Surrey had to make do with The Hon. Mrs. E.F. Bray. (It is of interest that none of these ladies insisted on being called 'chairlady' or 'chairperson'.)

Many girls of Epsom and Ewell joined the W.L.A. and some of them worked on local farms and smallholdings. At one stage of the war the girls would meet at Epsom Clocktower

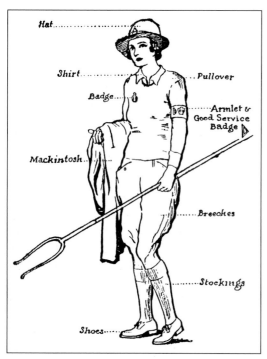

85 Regulation dress of a Land Army girl.

86 The Local Home Guard was of the 56th Surrey Battalion. This shows the East Surrey 'H.Q.' Platoon in October 1944.

and be taken by lorry to their places of work. A proposal to plough up The Hill on Epsom Race Course was not proceeded with in the face of local objections and the unsuitability of the chalk soil for cultivation.

Something like 80,000 girls joined the W.L.A. throughout the country and they made a big contribution to the effort that brought about a 1943 harvest that was twice the pre-war figure.

As part of the war effort numerous small 'shadow factories' were set up to manufacture components to feed the large factories making armaments and munitions. Locations of these shadow factories in Epsom included South Street, Dorking Road, Pitt Road and Ashley Avenue.

Men from 17 to 65 years of age not already in the forces joined the Local Defence Volunteers formed in mid-May 1940, when a

German invasion seemed inevitable. Their makeshift weapons were replaced by more effective ones after they became the Home Guard in July 1940. The local battalion was the 56th Surrey (Epsom & Banstead). They had numerous units in the borough: those in Epsom are thought to have included units located at Epsom Grand Stand, College Road, Woodcote Road, in the grounds of the RAC Club at Woodcote Park, Epsom College, Langley Vale, West Street and also at the Electricity Station in Depot Road and the Gas Works in East Street.

Members of the Home Guard from Epsom and Ewell manned four 3.7 inch anti-aircraft guns at Raynes Park. A company of the Welsh Guards that was stationed at Epsom Grandstand helped train the Home Guard as did Canadian troops that were stationed in the area.

Air Raids

Epsom and Ewell were sufficiently near London to attract bombs, and raids started in earnest soon after Dunkirk in June 1940, daylight raids being replaced by night-time bombing. The raids continued with varying degrees of intensity until the Allies invaded mainland Europe on 6 June 1944. However, attacks by conventional bombs were replaced by V-1 flying bombs, soon to be followed by the even more deadly V-2 rocket.

Damage by flying bombs included the destruction of the Ashley Road Police Station on 3 July 1944: temporary accommodation had to be used until 4 February 1946, when the police were able to move back into the rebuilt station. A new police station in Church Street became operative on 29 July 1963.

There is no precise record of the number of bombs that fell in Epsom and Ewell: there is wide variation in the reports. There were bombs of all types, including different sizes of H.E. bombs, parachute mines, incendiary and anti-personnel (butterfly) bombs as well as large oil incendiary bombs. It is thought that there could have been as many as 440 H.E. bombs, 40 or so of which failed to explode, and which would have been dealt with by the bomb disposal squads of the Royal Engineers. Many of the H.E. and incendiary bombs fell during the night blitzes of 1940-1. The total number of bombs was probably something like 2,500 including some 30 V-1s.

A total of 890 'alerts' was sounded in the borough in the course of the war and 33 persons were killed by enemy action while hundreds were injured. Nearly 200 houses were destroyed and 12,000 damaged.

Life in war-time

In addition to the danger from bombing, life in war-time Epsom had many hardships and frustrations. It must have been galling for the many people who had recently acquired their first family car to have to lay it up on blocks in the garage for the duration of the war, as fuel was available for essential work only. There was the black-out to be endured: one had to get around with the dimmest of torches and cycle-lights. Cycling in unfamiliar districts was not helped by the absence of sign-posts: they had been taken down to confuse the enemy.

In January 1940 rationing of foods such as butter, meat, sugar and tea had been introduced: all foods were in short supply. Some people coped by keeping chickens and rabbits, and there was much bartering of supplies. Fortunately, babies and children were well looked after, with special allowances of milk, orange juice and cod liver oil. When reconstituted eggs began to arrive from America many interesting recipes were devised to make them more palatable than they might otherwise have been.

Life in the house was pretty dismal, as windows had to be blacked out, and the size of light-bulbs reduced. Although many of the houses damaged in air raids could still be lived in, they received only emergency repairs, which could leave them damp and draughty. Furthermore, coal was difficult to come by, and frequently there was no gas or electricity. People worked long hours, but still had to find time for fire-watching and A.R.P. duties. It was not easy when nights had to be spent in uncomfortable air-raid shelters.

But in spite of everything, people managed to snatch moments of enjoyment. Cinemas put on films when the danger from air raids was not too great and there were dances at public halls and some church halls. The radio provided entertainment as well as news. In fact, one elderly lady (who was a young lady during the war) is reported to have said: 'Epsom was good fun in the war, really. There was plenty to do, with three cinemas, the Capitol, the Odeon and the Cinema Royal. There were various dances including those at the Baths Hall. All the troops were there—the Canadians, the French Canadians, the Engineers and the R.A.F.'

Nevertheless, when the war in Europe came to an end on 8 May 1945 there was much rejoicing, with impromptu parades and street parties and lots of improvised red, white and blue bunting. There were further celebrations when the Second World War finally ended on 14 August 1945 with the surrender of Japan, but not on the same scale: it seemed more remote.

The war took the lives of nearly 300 service people from Epsom and Ewell.

Epsom After the Second World War

For several years after the war building work had to be confined to rebuilding houses that had been destroyed and repairing those that had been damaged. However, by the 1950s developers were able to get to work and many new houses were built. There had been some development of Langley Bottom, now known as Langley Vale, before the First World War and this had continued between the wars. It was mostly by individuals buying plots of land

and having houses built, rather than large-scale development. But it was after the Second World War that the main development of the area occurred. This piecemeal development has led to the half mile long by quarter mile wide enclave on the downs being composed of a mixture of houses: detached, semi-detached and bungalows, in a wide variety of designs.

The Wells estate on the Common tells a similar story. On the Ordnance Survey map of 1895 the area that had been cleared on the common around the Well is largely free of houses, apart from the large house, The Wells, although there had been some small houses built just outside the circle along what became Woodlands Road. By 1932 The Greenway with a few houses along it had appeared in the circle, but it was not until after the Second World War that the Wells estate was built up to the extent that it is now.

There have been times since the end of the Second World War when there was a danger of Epsom and Ewell being merged with

87 Efforts were made to bring life back to normal as quickly as possible after the War. In 1946 there was a concert given in Epsom Baths Hall by the Surrey Philharmonic Orchestra with soprano Elizabeth Schumann.

88 As can be seen from this 1954 photograph, at that time there were still a few gaps in the High Street. The building on the right is the *Charter Inn*, which replaced the *Railway Inn* that was demolished during the road widening of the 1930s. The *Charter Inn* closed and was converted to shops in 1971.

89 The onset of the 'Cold War' made air-raid precautions necessary and Epsom and Ewell had its C.D. Corps. This shows a training exercise in July 1958.

90 The housing development at Langley Vale has led to an enclave in a hollow on the Downs.

91 The Langley Vale Church, known as St Stephen's Epsom Downs, was built in 1961 and replaced a 'tin' mission church.

adjacent boroughs and losing its identity, one of the most serious attacks on the borough being the London Government Bill of 1962, which would have made it part of the London area. The council vigorously opposed the proposals, ably led by the Town Clerk, Edward Moore, who had been appointed in 1945. Edward Moore had also worked to ensure that the Epsom parliamentary constituency should remain intact when it was under threat in 1946 and in 1954. In recognition of his efforts he was granted the honorary freedom of the borough in 1963. More recently, proposals to make Epsom and Ewell a Unitary Authority have also been rejected.

One of the most important events in recent years has been the building of the Ashley Centre. In the early 1970s it was considered that development was needed to revitalise Epsom and to establish it as a major shopping centre. The area between Ashley Avenue and the High Street was identified as the best location and this was embodied in the County Development Plan of 1974 following a Public Inquiry. The brief prepared for developers in 1977 laid down the areas of floorspace required for shops and offices, a minimum of 800 parking spaces, a replacement for the Ebbisham and Myers Halls (in Ashley Road) that were to be demolished, and a cinema. Ashley Avenue, then a cul-de-sac, was to be taken through to South Street to become part of the A24.

The shopping centre that was opened by the Queen on 24 October 1984 included five major stores, 39 shop units and 14 specialist boutiques. There was a multi-storey car park with 800 parking spaces, an office block and multi-purpose halls (The Playhouse and Myers Hall).

92   Queen Elizabeth II visited Epsom in June 1977, her Jubilee year.

93 The Centre of Epsom was transformed by the building of the Ashley Shopping Centre, following a brief prepared for developers in 1977. This shows work in progress on 5 July 1982.

94 The Ashley Centre was opened on 24 October 1984 by the Queen. Here she is seen signing the visitors' book.

Schools

One result of the war was the decision not to use the Hook Road boys school for a while as it had no air-raid shelter, so some of the boys were accommodated in the Ladbroke Road School with the girls, and Church House by St Martin's Church was brought into use, while other boys were transferred to Pound Lane School. Church House also took in children from the Hawthorne Place Infants School which was destroyed in a night time air raid in October 1940. Many Epsom children were evacuated, some even going as far as Cornwall. The Chief Billeting Officer of the Camelford Rural Area reported that local people were impressed by the 'niceness' of the Epsom children.

As a result of the 1944 Education Act the Epsom County School for boys became Epsom Grammar School and fees were abolished. In 1953 it was renamed Glyn Grammar School. Hook Road boys school came back into use and continued to function until it closed in 1964 after new schools had been built.

There was a wholesale re-organisation of the schools in Epsom when the borough had to 'go comprehensive' in 1976. The Hessle Grove school retained its identity as a boys' school, Glyn School, and in 1994 it became Glyn/ADT School of Technology.

The Epsom School of Art and Design which had started life in the Technical Institute acquired new premises in Ashley Road in 1973. The old building in Church Street is still in use today for evening and other part-time classes.

Chapter Ten

The Mental Hospitals

A major event at the end of the 19th century that went on long into the next century was the building of a large complex of mental hospitals to the north west of Epsom in what had been the manor of Horton, a complex known in recent years as the Hospitals Cluster. The London County Council, at its formation in 1888, found itself responsible for the care of thousands of mentally ill people. Its solution was to buy in 1896 a large estate in the Surrey countryside and build a number of enormous asylums on the most progressive lines. The recent owners of Horton Estate had had problems that made them anxious to sell and the L.C.C. were able to buy at £35,900, a bargain for an estate that included the manor house with its gardens and woodland, together with five farms: Home Farm, New Farm, Horton Farm, Greenman Farm and West Farm.

Plans were made for six hospitals with a total population of 12,000, although only five were actually built. The first was known as Horton Manor Asylum and it opened for patients in 1899. Because of the pressing need

95 Horton Manor House was incorporated in the Administrative Offices of Horton Manor Asylum, which opened in 1899.

96 The administration block of Horton Asylum, with the water/observation tower behind.

97 View from Horton Asylum observation tower.

98 The Horton Asylum had a large recreation hall.

for accommodation, it was built as temporary units around Horton Manor House, in which staff were housed, and initially provision was made for 700 women patients. Some of the temporary units were still in use more than 80 years later.

There was a little more time to build the next asylum, to be known as Horton, which opened in 1902. The design was by George Thomas Hine, who had already been responsible for Claybury and Bexley asylums and had developed a standard pattern involving a main semi-circular corridor with an administrative block in the middle and wards leading off it. Horton Asylum was built for two thousand

people. The heavy clay soil made problems for the builders, but it did have one advantage: it was suitable for brickmaking, and the bricks for Horton Hospital were made on site. This local gault clay gives a whitish brick. After the completion of the hospital railway in 1905, bricks were brought in.

Horton Asylum was followed by Ewell Epileptic Colony, later known as St Ebba's, which opened in 1904, followed by Long Grove Asylum in 1907. The First World War delayed the building programme, and it was not until 1924 that West Park Hospital opened. Horton, Long Grove and West Park were built to the semi-circular plan, while Manor and

99 Patients were encouraged to take the air in 'airing courts'.

100 Horton also had a large chapel.

101 Nurses of 'K' Ward, Manor Asylum, *c.*1910.

St Ebba's were to irregular plans with dispersed buildings.

There was no shortage of patients to fill the wards of these hospitals: following the 1890 Lunacy Act, parish Poor Law Guardians saved 60 per cent of their costs if they referred someone to an asylum, rather than keeping them in the workhouse; furthermore, doctors were paid a fee for each person they certified, so the mentally disturbed were seldom given the benefit of the doubt. Having an illegitimate child could be regarded as abnormal behaviour that was certifiable, while some of those committed were suffering from nothing worse than depression. The system was weighted against women as they had less defence in law than men and in the early days of the hospitals there were far more women inmates than men.

The asylums/hospitals were well organised and strictly regimented: many doctors and nurses did their best to cure or alleviate the suffering of their patients, and a full range of amenities was provided, including a large chapel and a concert hall where inmates and staff would work together to put on performances. For some patients music was provided as a therapy. The hospitals developed as caring communities which were in many respects self sufficient, with their own workshops and farms that supplied most of the required vegetables. They were surrounded by well-tended parkland.

In the First World War, in February 1915 Horton Asylum was taken over by the War Office; its 2,143 patients were moved elsewhere and arrangements were made to receive wounded soldiers. By the time Horton closed as a military hospital in 1919, more than 44,000 servicemen had been treated. Manor Asylum and St Ebba's also had some use as military hospitals.

Horton was again evacuated in the Second World War and adapted for use as an Emergency Medical Service hospital for both civilian and military casualties, which took service-men after Dunkirk and D-Day.

The Hospital Railway

When contractors started work on Long Grove Asylum they had problems conveying building materials from the London, Brighton and South Coast Railway Station at Epsom over what were largely country lanes, using horses and carts and some steam traction. Their solution was to apply to the Board of Trade for permission to build a railway, and this was granted in July 1905. The Long Grove Railway was built to carry the supplies from a siding at Ewell West Station to the site of the hospital and was for the most part within the grounds of the hospitals' complex. The standard gauge single-line system was completed in 1905 and was operated initially by one and later by two small tank engines.

The railway clearly demonstrated its usefulness, because, when work on Long Grove was completed in 1907, the London County Council bought it to serve the future hospital at West Park and the Central Pumping and Electric Light Works newly-built near Horton Hospital. It was found to be best to replace the old railway with a new one taking a different route and provided with branch lines: this was brought into operation in 1913 and was called The Horton Light Railway. More attention was paid to safety than on the original line: all junctions with roads and paths were bridged and the lines were fenced. In 1906 an old lady had been run down and killed at Hook Road level-crossing on the old railway.

After the building of West Park, the main cargo carried on the railway was coal for heating, some 15,000 tonnes a year brought in 12-ton wagons from sidings at Raynes Park. The Horton Light Railway went out of use in 1950, by which time road transport was considered more efficient. The track was taken up, but its route can be traced over much of its length as a bridleway in Horton Country Park.

The Hospitals after the Second World War
The Second World War was followed by changes in the care and treatment of the mentally ill. Residential care began to be replaced by treatment at day centres. Antidepressant and tranquilliser drugs became available and could be prescribed by G.P.s so there was less need for hospital admissions. For those who were in mental hospitals, the regime became less rigid: a process of de-institutionalising began.

In 1961 the Minister of Health, Enoch Powell, announced that he intended to close most of the country's mental hospitals. It was a somewhat premature decision, because little work had been done on care in the community and its funding, and it was to be some 20 years before closures began in earnest. Proposals for closing some of the Epsom hospitals were

formulated in 1983, and alternative arrangements for looking after patients were investigated.

Long Grove closed in 1992, The Manor in 1996 and Horton in 1998. At the time of writing St Ebba's is being run down preparatory to closing. Parts are to be retained for hospital use. West Park buildings are still intact. The New Cottage Hospital at West Park is in new buildings.

Most of the hospital sites will be developed for housing, mostly by building new houses after demolition of the old buildings. What is envisaged for the Epsom Hospitals Cluster is virtually a new town with some 1,500 dwellings; new roads are being built to link the planned housing complexes together and to Epsom. The Horton Hospital site will become the centre of this new community and an attempt will be made to create a village atmosphere. Horton Chapel, which is a Listed Building, will be put to community use for concerts and theatrical performances. A shuttle bus service to Epsom town centre will be provided.

Horton Chapel is not the only building to be retained: several conservation areas have been set up to preserve some of the more interesting buildings, and there will be a degree of conversion into housing units. The conservation area for The Manor will include the administrative building that contains part of Horton Place, the Horton manor house dating from the early 19th century. Parts of the Central Boilerhouse are to be conserved.

As early as 1973 the farms of West Park and Long Grove became surplus to the needs of these hospitals and were purchased by Epsom and Ewell Borough Council to become Horton Country Park, containing a golf course, equestrian centre and a demonstration farm for children. The remaining open spaces of fields, hedgerows, woods and ponds are also for public enjoyment. With the closure of the hospitals, more land will be taken into the Country Park.

Chapter Eleven

The Races

The open downland that stretched from Croydon above the villages of Wallington and Carshalton and over Banstead and Epsom Downs was covered with fine turf and was ideal for racing. John Toland referred to the Downs as 'being covered with grass finer than Persian carpets, and perfumed with wild thyme and juniper ... for sheep-walks, riding, hunting, racing, shooting, with games of most sorts for exercise of the body or recreation of the mind ... they are no where else to be paralleled.'

There was horse racing on the Downs at an early date: in the 1580s Queen Elizabeth I went several times to a horse race near Croydon when she was staying at the Archbishop of Canterbury's palace in that town. Racing also took place around 1610 when James I was in residence at Nonsuch Palace and it was certainly well established some 50 years later when in his diary Pepys recorded that 'horse races took place daily at noon, and cudgel-playing, wrestling, hawking and foot racing in the afternoon'.

There was much informal horse racing on the Downs, including the original steeple-chasing, in which 'two horsemen, drunk or sober, in or out of their wits, fix upon a steeple or some other conspicuous distant object, to which they make a straight cut, over hedge, ditch and gate'.

When formal racing developed it bore little resemblance to present ideas of a horse race such as The Derby: it was a trial of stamina rather than speed, and was run on a four-mile straight course from Carshalton to Epsom Downs, or as straight as the hilly terrain would allow. The result was decided by several heats being run. Horses were rubbed down between heats in a wooden shed that has given its name to *The Rubbing House* public house within the present Epsom race-course, said to be the only public house on a race-course.

When John Toland wrote his account of Epsom in 1711 he referred to 'the new orbicular race' and also 'the four-mile course over the Warrenhouse to Carshalton', so it would appear that both courses were in use at that time.

Eclipse

An event that was to have a considerable effect on racing at Epsom, and indeed on racing throughout the world, was the birth in 1764 at the Duke of Cumberland's stud in Windsor Great Park of a remarkable horse that was foaled during the great eclipse of 1 April 1764 and so was named 'Eclipse', an ungainly looking animal and bad tempered: he was sold off to a William Wildman, who sent him to a horse-breaker at Epsom.

It was discovered that Eclipse was fast and of great stamina, but he was not entered for a race until he was five years old in 1769. At the start of the race a backer pronounced that the result would be 'Eclipse first, the rest nowhere' meaning that he would outdistance the rest of the field by 240 yards, and that is what happened. After more easy wins Eclipse was bought for 1750 guineas by Dennis O'Kelly,

102   Both the Prince's Stand and *The Rubbing House* pub can be seen in this photograph taken from the Queen's Stand.

who entered him for nine races in 1770, all of which he won. Other owners would not enter horses against him, and so Eclipse was retired to O'Kelly's stud at Clay Hill, Epsom and made a fortune in fees. Eclipse was such a successful sire that in 1906 it was estimated that 82 out of 127 Derby winners were his descendants. O'Kelly erected what has been described as a beautiful and elegant villa at Clay Hill (now West Hill), and entertained there the élite of the racing world.

The Oaks and The Derby

The two races that have made Epsom famous came about because of the 12th Earl of Derby who, when he succeeded to the title in 1776, acquired great wealth and numerous estates. He spent much of his time at The Oaks, a house set in extensive parkland in the parish of Woodmansterne near Carshalton on the northern slopes of the open downland.

Lord Derby, the 12th Earl, was a great sportsman, with a particular interest in horse-racing and cock-fighting. Race-meetings were organised on the downland near The Oaks. As a patron of cock-fighting, he was one of the most famous in England and is said to have owned three thousand gamecocks at one time. His passion for the sport was such that he had a cock-pit installed in the dining-room at The Oaks under a hinged section of the floor.

Lord Derby entertained many of his sporting friends at The Oaks and, at a dinner after a race-meeting in May 1778, they began to discuss initiating a race that would be different from the ones consisting of heats run over two or four miles. The result was the decision to establish a new race on the course on Epsom Downs the following year. It was to be a race for three-year-old fillies over a distance of one and a half miles, and there was general

103   The Prince's Stand was the first permanent grandstand. It was rebuilt in 1879.

agreement that it should be called The Oaks, as that was where it had been invented.

The first Oaks run in 1779 was won by Lord Derby's filly, Bridget. The new race was such a great success that, at the dinner at The Oaks following the event, Derby and his friends came up with the idea for another race, a short race of one mile only that would be for three-year-old colts as well as fillies. Derby suggested that the new race should be named 'The Bunbury' after Sir Charles Bunbury, President of the Jockey Club, who was present at the dinner. Bunbury was the racing authority of the day and a moving force behind the idea of shorter races to replace the laborious two- and four-mile events. Others thought that 'The Derby' would be more appropriate, and this is what it became; according to tradition, the matter was decided on the toss of a coin, and thus came about the most famous horse-race in the world.

The first Derby run was on Epsom Downs on 4 May 1780, and it was won by Sir Charles

Bunbury's horse, Diomed, ridden by Sam Arnull. It was not until 1787 that one of Lord Derby's horses, Sir Peter Teazle, won the race, the length of which had been increased to one and a half miles in 1784.

Lord Derby was at The Oaks until shortly before his death in 1834. The largely 18th-century house suffered bomb damage and deterioration in the Second World War and was later demolished. Fortunately The Oaks estate had been made part of the Green Belt and much of it has been retained as public parkland.

The Grand Stand

Apart from the little Prince's stand built towards the end of the 18th century there was no permanent grandstand until 1830; temporary erections of wood and canvas were put up for race days. (The Prince's stand was rebuilt in 1879.)

An entrepreneur, Charles Bluck from Doncaster, was able to obtain from John

Briscoe, M.P., lord of the manor of Epsom, a lease of one acre of the Downs for 90 years from 25 March 1829 at £30 a year, his plan being to build a grandstand in brick or stone on which he would spend at least £5,000. However, a group of local gentlemen had a grander scheme in mind, and quickly formed an Epsom Grand Stand Association with proposals to build a stand for 5,000 spectators. It was their intention to raise £20,000 from 1,000 shares at £20 each. They offered Bluck £1,000 to sub-let his lease, which he accepted, subject to being allowed to lease four rooms on the ground floor of the new building. The Association soon got to work, and appointed an architect, Edward William Trendall. Part of his contract was that for an additional fee of 10 guineas he was to make a drawing of the new grandstand for King George IV: the Association could see advantages of royal patronage for the Epsom races. After further sharp, at times acrimonious, negotiations, Charles Bluck assigned the main lease to the EGSA and work on the stand quickly progressed, so that, although not complete, they were able to use it for the 1830 Derby. At that time there were two meetings a year, one in the week before Whitsun and

104 A share certificate for the grandstand that was completed in 1830. There were to be 1,000 shares at £20.

105 The grandstand in 1835.

106   Crowds returning from the Derby through Epsom High Street in 1906.

one in October. The Oaks and The Derby came in the earlier meeting.

The new grandstand had been conceived on a grand scale: 2,000 of the 5,000 spectators were accommodated on the roof. It had a pillared hall and a saloon 110 feet long. There were four refreshment rooms, kitchens and a warren of committee and retiring rooms.

The popularity of The Derby

The great popularity of racing at Epsom and in particular The Derby was due to a number of factors, not the least of which was its nearness to London, the most thriving, bustling city in the world, full of lively, boisterous citizens eager for entertainment, and this the

races on the Downs could offer. What better venue for people to get together than that open chalk downland: the fine turf that made the going good for horses was also ideal for picnics. There was ample space for tents and booths, so that in race weeks the Downs became a tented city, a vast fairground, where every possible diversion was on offer. There were musicians, dancing girls, jugglers, tumblers, fortune tellers, conjurers, clowns and sword swallowers. There were vendors of fruit, pies, gingerbread, sweets, trinkets and anything else that could be dispensed by itinerant traders.

In the days when public holidays were rare events, going to The Derby became a long anticipated treat comparable to Christmas. Factory workers would set up payment clubs so that they could save up to enable them to hire a coach and do The Derby in style in their best clothes.

As early as 1793 Derby Day meant crowded roads, and *The Times* reported that 'the road to Epsom was crowded with all descriptions of people hurrying to the races, some to plunder and some to be plundered. Horses, gigs, curricles, coaches, chaises, carts and pedestrians, covered with dust, crowded the Downs.'

Watching the traffic, the unbroken lines of vehicles of all description making their way out of London, became an entertainment in itself and the influx of strangers was a cause of concern to towns and villages on the route. The appointment by Sutton Vestry of three special constables to protect the village during the 1838 Epsom Race Week is typical. Epsom town too was thronged with crowds of people during the race weeks, particularly on Derby Day, and the streets were fumigated for fear of infection.

The estimated number of people attending the Derby in 1843 was in excess of 127,000, and it would have been nearer 200,000 in the second half of the 19th century. Although the numbers have dropped in recent years, figures as high as 110,000 have been estimated.

The indefatigable social investigator, Henry Mayhew, in *London Labour and the London Poor*, published in 1851, gave an amusing account of an interview with a street conjurer who went out to Epsom races and was able to extract as much as £6 from wealthy punters with his performances.

Royal patronage has played its part in the fashionable appeal of Epsom and The Derby. Although Queen Victoria made only the 1840 visit, Prince Edward, later King Edward VII, gave his support. His horses won The Derby in 1896, 1900 and 1909. Later monarchs also were Derby goers: our present Queen seldom misses the event.

Radio and television have spread the word so that Epsom and The Derby are part of the national consciousness. Jockeys may not have quite the pulling power of pop and football stars, but few apart from the very young will fail to recognise such names as Fred Archer, Charlie Smirke, Steve Donoghue, Willy Carson and Lester Piggot.

107 Lord Rosebery with 'Ladas'. See Chapter Thirteen.

108 Tom Walls with 'April 5th'. See Chapter Thirteen.

The Dorlings

For much of the 19th century and well into the 20th racing in Epsom was dominated by the Dorling family. William Dorling, a printer in Bexhill, moved to Epsom in about 1820 and established a business with a printing press in a large house at what is now the junction of East Street and Upper High Street.

By 1830 he was printing almanacks, hymn books and above all Dorling's Genuine Card List which gave Derby runners, owners, jockeys, colours and horse pedigrees. The List first went on sale for the 1827 Derby, and was an instant success. Dorling's shop sold not only printed material, but also many other items that racegoers might require, including writing paper, shaving soap and lavender water. William's activities brought him into contact with many racing personalities. He and his son Henry attended the inaugural meeting of the Epsom Grand Stand Association and bought shares in the concern. In 1839 Henry was appointed Clerk of the Course. Both the Dorlings had other involvement in the life of Epsom: William was the registrar of births and deaths and Henry was deputy registrar.

Although The Derby attracted more and more people every year, not enough of them were going into the grandstand. They were presumably put off by the entrance fee of 5s. The Association relied on the grandstand for its income and the situation was a cause of concern. Profit was low; in fact some years there was a deficit. A visit by Queen Victoria in 1840 boosted attendance at the grandstand that year by 25 per cent, and this enabled the committee to pay out four per cent to shareholders.

In 1841 the committee came to the conclusion that it might do better to let the stand to a businessman who could run it at a profit and Henry Dorling agreed to take it on a 21-year lease. He immediately put forward detailed proposals for improving racing at Epsom, including enlarging the lawn in front of the stand and providing better accommodation for jockeys and stewards—changes that marked the start of a period of increased efficiency in the conduct of racing and a growing prestige.

In 1846 another new race was introduced, the Great Metropolitan Handicap, at one time known as 'The Publicans' Derby' because initially the prize-money was put up by London publicans, many of whose pubs served as betting shops. The Great Met started in front of the stands going the reverse way down the home straight before branching off onto an 'S' shaped course marked out on the Downs that rejoined the Derby track on the far side before returning via Tattenham Corner. In 1985 the 'S' shaped course over the Downs was abandoned for safety reasons and the Derby course is now utilised for the race, the distance being reduced from two miles and two furlongs to one and a half miles.

The new race was so successful that in 1851 another new race, the City and Suburban, was introduced into the Epsom programme, with prize-money raised from the pubs not only of the City of London, but of the suburbs also. It used the Derby course, but with the length reduced to one mile and two furlongs.

109 William Dorling came to Epsom in about 1820 and established a printing business at the junction of East Street and Station Road (now Upper High Street), seen here in this early photograph. In the left background can be seen the engine shed in which the railway terminated.

110 William Dorling's son Henry became Clerk of the Course of Epsom Race Course and played a prominent part in its development.

After an absence of seven years, in 1997 the two races were revived at the re-instigated Spring Meeting.

In consultation with Lord George Bentinck, a respected racing authority, Henry Dorling introduced an important change in 1847. The start of the mile and a half Derby course was high on The Hill behind Downs House and was out of sight of the stands. The start was moved to the other side of Downs House in full view of the stands. Being lower down The Hill meant that the horses were faced with a stiff uphill pull of several furlongs before joining the old course at Tattenham Corner, and a sharper turn, but it was considered that the benefit of being able to see the start from the stands outweighed the disadvantages. (There was a further change in 1872 to a higher starting point and it has remained there to this day.) The present course involves a climb of about 135 feet to the high part at the hill, a

drop of 96 feet to the 100-yard marker followed by a rise of three feet to the winning post.

By 1847 The Derby had become so popular that on 18 May that year Lord George Bentinck proposed the adjournment of the House of Commons until the Thursday, a practice that continued throughout most of the second half of the 19th century. (It may be wondered how a lord could sit in the House of Commons: although of noble descent, a son of the fourth Duke of Portland, and popularly known as Lord George Bentinck, he was not actually a lord.)

Henry Dorling had married Emily Clarke, who had four children before she died. In 1843 he married Elizabeth Mayson, a widow with four children, bringing Henry's family up to eight children. Henry and Elizabeth then produced 13 children, giving a total of 21, which was a large family, even by Victorian standards. By 1845 there were nine children to be

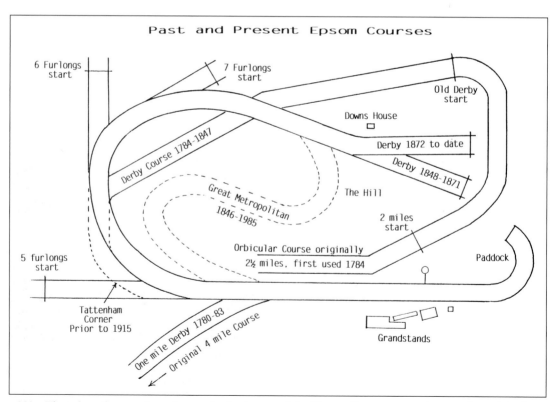

111   There have been various changes in the layout of the Epsom Course, as can be seen from this plan.

accommodated, and the house at the end of what is now Upper High Street had become somewhat overcrowded. Elizabeth had a solution: the children could live in the Grand Stand, looked after by the grandmother. The Grand Stand, with its committee and retiring rooms and kitchens, had been fitted out with luxurious carpets and wallpaper for the visit of Queen Victoria in 1840, and offered ideal accommodation for a large family. Well, perhaps not ideal: they had to move out with their belongings when there were race meetings. Furthermore, although life in the Grand Stand was very pleasant in the summer, it was less so in winter, as it was impossible to keep it warm. However, there the children lived until they were sent away to boarding schools.

With so many children running around, even the Grand Stand was noisy at times, leading to the famous occasion when Henry called out—'For heaven's sake, Elizabeth, what is all that noise about?' 'That, Henry, is your children and my children fighting our children.'

112 Mr. Dearle, an Epsom tallowchandler, did not miss a single Derby. This shows him returning from his 80th Derby.

113 Henry Mayson Dorling succeeded his father as Clerk of the Course and came to be regarded as the dictator of Epsom racing.

114 The grandstand and the crowds, Derby Day, 1895.

When his lease expired Henry Dorling continued to run things as a joint managing director of the EGSA and, when he died in 1873, the Association was in a much stronger financial position than it had been. His success owed much to his naturally persuasive manner and personal charm.

There was another Dorling waiting in the wings, Henry Mayson Dorling, Henry's son by his first marriage. Henry Mayson was appointed Clerk of the Course in succession to his father, and later Chairman and Joint Managing Director. In 1886 they had the Grand Stand enlarged and refitted under the direction of Hatchard Smith.

As Clerk of the Course, Chairman of the Committee and Joint Managing Director, Henry Mayson Dorling had even more power than his father, and was not afraid to exercise it: he has often been referred to as the Dictator of Epsom Races. A more detailed comment is that he was a true martinet, a self-assured, uncompromising dictator, capable of fighting tooth and nail against anyone. He had no illusions about what others thought of him, and is reported to have boasted: 'Everyone hates me, and I like it.' He died in 1919 at the age of 84.

A significant achievement of Henry Mayson Dorling was in 1888 when he was able to acquire for the Association a large part of the Walton estate, described as: '205 acres of boldly undulating land including the famous galloping or training ground for flat races distinguished as Six Mile Hill and a portion of the Derby Racecourse adjacent to the far-famed Tattenham Corner.'

Epsom races in the 20th Century

The 20th century saw significant changes in the organisation of racing at Epsom. In 1925, Stanley Wootton bought from the Association a large part of the land that had been acquired from the Walton Estate, including Six Mile Hill, and ran The Gallops as a commercial operation. Wootton was a wealthy farmer and race-horse trainer of Australian origin. The £35,000 he paid helped the Association to buy the freehold of their Epsom land from Epsom Manor.

Work started in 1926 on the construction of new grandstands following demolition of the old one. It was to be done between the end of the Derby meeting and the start of the following spring meeting, a period of 10 months. There were problems in the form of the General Strike and the effect it had on the British Steel Industry: the steel girders required could not be obtained in time and supplies from the Continent had to be sought. The builders made a tremendous effort to get the job done in spite of the unforeseen delays, and by employing something like 500 men working round the clock were able to have the stands partially ready for the spring meeting, able to accommodate 12,000 spectators, rather than the full number of 20,000. When completed, the new stands comprised an open, single tier at the east end, a large central stand surmounted by more than 200 private boxes, each with its own bar and luncheon room, and on the west the Club Stand which included accommodation for royalty, who could view the races from a wide terrace.

115 Derby Day attracted a multitude of vendors, as can be seen in this 1910 photograph.

116 The new grandstand, shortly after completion in 1927.

117 Gypsies were long a feature of the Epsom scene; they were not always popular with the authorities, who in 1937 prohibited them from going onto the Downs. Their champion, Lady Sybil Grant, who was living at The Durdans, allowed the Gypsies to use one of her fields.

118-19 The grandstands just prior to the building of the Queen's Stand and after building it.

James Chuter Ede, long active in politics at local, county and national level, put forward in the House of Commons a bill which was passed in 1936 as 'The Epsom and Walton Downs Regulation Act'. The Act established a body of Conservators, whose first duty was 'to preserve the Downs as far as possible in their natural state of beauty with due regard to the rules of good forestry'. They were given powers to make by-laws and the authority to see that they were enforced. The rights of the EGSA were recognised, i.e., the right to maintain its buildings and to control access to the race-courses on racing days. Stanley Wootton was allowed to maintain the training gallops on Walton Downs. The Act took away comm-oners' rights to graze animals on the Downs and provided appropriate compensation.

In 1959 the open stand at the east end of the complex was demolished and in its place was built the Rosebery stand.

1961 saw the creation of the Horserace Betting Levy Board, which was concerned not only with raising money by a tax on betting, but also promoting the improvement of race-courses and it was to play an important part in racing at Epsom. In 1964 the Board helped EGSA purchase the freehold of the paddock from the Durdans estate, as well as subsidising the construction of the pedestrian tunnel and

the building of stables. United Racecourses Ltd. was set up as a holding company for EGSA in 1965. In 1969 Stanley Wootton gave the Walton Downs gallops to the Levy Board and they were also able to acquire Epsom Downs, so that today both Epsom Downs and Walton Downs are administered for the benefit of the public.

The grandstand complex that occupies such a prominent position on the Downs acquired a new look in 1992 with the completion of the Queen's Stand that replaced the Club Stand.

Emily Davison

There was a dramatic event during the 1913 Derby when suffragette Emily Davison, in the words of the coroner, 'was accidentally knocked down by a horse through wilfully rushing onto the racecourse'. She suffered a fractured skull and died on 10 June 1913 in Epsom Cottage Hospital. It is doubtful whether there was much support for the suffragettes in Epsom. In 1908 local dignitary Basil Braithwaite read a paper on women's suffrage in which he said: 'The real answer to the question "Why should not a woman have the vote" is a very simple one: "because she is a woman—and therefore has no right to trench on the prerogative of man, and indeed is unfitted to do so."'

120 The Queen's Stand, 1995.

Chapter Twelve

The Old Buildings of Epsom

The Spa, the races and the easy access to London encouraged wealthy people to build substantial houses in Epsom as main residences, summer houses or as property for letting as an investment; as a result, the town is richer in Late Stuart, Queen Anne and Georgian houses than any other place in Surrey. Some London merchants would live with their families in their Epsom home during the summer, driving up to Town every morning.

The original Epsom village grew around the Church, but Church Street became a fashionable area in which many large houses were built, leaving nothing of the pre-Spa buildings except for the small house number 45, sometimes known as The Hermitage, the earliest part of which has been dated at around 1600. *The Old King's Head* opposite the Church is *c.*1660. Before the Spa period the great houses were Woodcote Park and The Durdans.

Woodcote Park

Woodcote Park had been enclosed in the manor of Horton, and came into the possession of Elizabeth, the eldest daughter of George Mynne, as part of the manor. She married Richard Evelyn in 1648 and he built a new mansion at Woodcote. It is said to have included decorative work by Grinling Gibbons and Antonio Verrio, done at the suggestion of Richard's brother John, the diarist. (Verrio was born in Naples in 1634 and was brought to England by Charles II to paint some of the ceilings at Hampton Court, where he died in 1707.) On the death of Elizabeth in 1692 Woodcote Park passed to Charles, third Lord Baltimore.

There is some uncertainty about the subsequent building history of the Woodcote Park mansion, but it seems highly probable that the 17th-century mansion was rebuilt at

121 The building in Church Street known as The Hermitage, parts of which have been dated to around 1600.

122 Woodcote Park Mansion built around 1750. This shows it in 1911 before it was destroyed by fire, after which it was rebuilt with a façade having an external appearance a close copy of the original. Copyright: Surrey History Service.

the time of Frederick, the 6th Lord Baltimore, in the French rococo style to the designs of Isaac Ware, incorporating elements of the old house such as the Verrio ceiling. It is known that building work was in progress in 1753. After the estate was sold by the 6th Lord (sometimes erroneously referred to as the 7th Lord Baltimore) in 1768 there were several subsequent owners and in 1787 it was acquired by Mr. Lewis Teissier, a London merchant, by which time the estate had been separated from the manor of Horton. Teissier's son, who owned Woodcote Park soon after the beginning of the 19th century, was created Baron de Teissier by the French King Louis XVIII. The Baron enriched the interior of the mansion with a decor to fit the current idea of the Louis Quinze style before he sold

the estate in 1856 to Robert Brooks. His son, a Director of the Bank of England, sold Woodcote Park to the Royal Automobile Club in 1913, for use as their country club. The building was destroyed by fire on 1 August 1934 and the Verrio ceiling and painted rooms were lost, except for the carved woodwork and panelling of a drawing room. They had been purchased in 1927 by the Museum of Fine Arts at Boston, Massachusetts. The RAC immediately rebuilt the house with a façade having an external appearance a close copy of the building that had been destroyed. The front steps together with arches and balustrading that link the two surviving wing buildings to the old mansion survived the fire. Also, it was possible to re-use some of the ornamental stonework of the façade.

123 The Drawing Room of Woodcote Park Mansion in 1911. Copyright: Surrey History Service.

124 The Dovecote of Woodcote Park dates back to the time of Richard Evelyn, *c.*1660.

The Durdans

The Durdans in Chalk Lane is a remnant of a large building much of which was built in 1764. (The Durdans estate is considered to be the property that included 12 acres of land with meadow, pasture and wood which was conveyed to Elizabeth, Lady Berkeley, by the lord of Horton manor in 1617.) There had been previous houses on the site; the one immediately before the present one was built by Lord Berkeley in the 1680s. It was the time of the demolition of Nonsuch Palace and a lot of the materials went into Durdans. Since Lord Berkeley had been Keeper of the Palace, it would have been no problem for him to acquire the stones. Durdans had some illustrious owners, including Lord North, Lord of the Bedchamber to Frederick, Prince of Wales, son of George II. Lord North loaned Durdans to the prince for a period around 1740 after he had been evicted from St James' Palace by his father. Frederick died in 1751, and so did not come to the throne. His eldest son became George III.

In 1747 Durdans was acquired by Alderman Belchier. He had Berkeley's house pulled down but the new one he had built burnt down in 1755. The shell was bought by Charles Dalbiac and rebuilt in 1764 by William Newton. In 1819 Sir Gilbert Heathcote bought Durdans. He was a member of the Jockey Club and active in the training and breeding of race horses. He won the Derby in 1838 with Amato, which was trained at Epsom. The Durdans estate stretched up to the race-course, in fact the paddock and parade ring came in the estate.

Lord Rosebery, the 5th Earl, bought the estate in 1874 in order to be near Epsom in the hope that it would help him to achieve his life long ambition to win The Derby, which he did in 1894 when he was Prime Minister. Lord Rosebery had extensive alterations made to the house, involving changing the position of the entrance to the opposite side of the house.

Lady Sybil Grant, daughter of the 5th Earl, inherited Durdans for life and lived there after the death of her father in 1929. She had a passionate interest in and sympathy for gypsies, and, when on one occasion the authorities wanted to clear them from the Downs, they had to back down when Lady Sybil threatened to stop the use of the paddock and parade ring. Lord Irwin, a nephew of Lord Rosebery, inherited the house in 1955, and had a large

125 The Durdans, completed in 1764. A large part of the house, including later additions, was demolished in the late 1950s.

126 In the grounds of The Durdans are the graves of several Derby winners, including that of 'Amato', who won the race in 1838.

127 Lord Rosebery had an indoor riding school in the grounds of The Durdans built by architect George Devey.

part of it demolished to make it more manageable.

One of Lord Rosebery's favourite flowers was the snowdrop and he had a spinney on the estate planted with them. He had been a patron of the Lest We Forget Association that was set up to help disabled soldiers and sailors, the Epsom, Ewell and District branch being formed in 1924. In 1932 Lady Sybil Grant proposed that snowdrops should be picked and sold in aid of the Association, a practice that continues today. At times, Durdans was the venue for events organised to raise funds for the Association.

In the grounds of Durdans is an indoor riding school built in 1881 by the architect George Devey, the roof construction of which,

with wide single-span timber trusses, is something rather special for that period.

The building of the Spa town
The development of the Spa town began in the High Street. Pepys refers to *The Kings Head* in 1667 and *The Crown* (on the opposite side of the High Street) was there in 1688. *The Spread Eagle* (originally *The Black Spread Eagle*), is also late 17th-century. In 1692 came the Assembly Rooms (Waterloo House) and *The Magpie Inn* is thought to have been built soon after, while Livingstone's entertainment centre nearby opened in 1707.

Epsom in the Spa period was regarded as a boom town where there was money to be made and it attracted property speculators, a prime example of whom was Josiah Diston, a Director and Deputy Governor of the Bank of England, who acquired numerous properties and plots of land between 1710 and 1725. These included what is now Woodcote Grove, where he had the present house built. Further properties he was involved with were Richmond House (Beaumont Nursing Home) and Parkhurst (Park Place House) in Church Street as well as other houses and plots of land there. He also had interests in South Street, The Parade, East Street and Woodcote Green in Epsom.

There are about 170 listed buildings in Epsom of which some comprise two or more adjacent dwellings. Nearly 60 of these listed buildings were erected in the Spa period, i.e., between c.1660 to c.1725. Quite a few of the smaller buildings are in the western High Street: the mansions are in locations away from the town centre, such as Church Street, Chalk Lane, Woodcote Green and Dorking Road. Some of these listed buildings are illustrated in the following pages, including all the Grade II★ buildings except those which are featured elsewhere.

The Grade II★ Buildings of Epsom

128 & 129 The Cedars, Church Street. A late 17th-century house with later extensions. The façade is early 18th-century. In the mid-18th century the owners were the Mysters of Charterhouse Square, whose coat-of-arms appears in several places (the arms seen below are over a doorway). There is some fine interior decoration including a Rococo ceiling. The two large cedar trees that gave the house its name were blown down in 1987.

130 The Hylands, Dorking Road. A mid-18th-century house that incorporates part of a late 17th-century structure.

131 Hylands House, Dorking Road; an early 18th-century house. The two-storey canted bays were added later as was the mansard roof.

132 Woodcote Green House, Woodcote Green Road. A late 17th-century house re-fronted in the late 18th century.

133 Woodcote Grove, Chalk Lane was built in the early 18th century for Josiah Diston, and originally known as Mount Diston. There are good original interior details. The estate was purchased by Lord Rosebery in 1895 to prevent building by speculators that might have spoiled his view from The Durdans, and settled as a life trust upon his daughter Lady Peggy Primrose (The Marchioness of Crewe). In 1957 the estate was purchased by W.S. Atkins and Partners, the consulting engineers, who in 1963 established their technology park in the grounds. The founder, William Atkins, was knighted in 1976 for his services to industry and in 1982 was made an Honorary Freeman of the Borough of Epsom and Ewell.

134 Woodcote End House/Queen Anne House, Woodcote Road. A mid-18th-century house. To the right is the late 17th-/early 18th-century portion now called Queen Anne House.

Anti-clockwise from left:

135 Ebbisham House in Church Street, built in 1722 by William Woodford of Epsom. The wings were added in the early 1990s in a style similar to the original building.

136 Ashley House, Ashley Road. A house built in 1769 that takes its name from Mary Ashley who lived there for many years before her death in 1849 aged 90. The interior is richly decorated with Adam-style work. The drawing was done by J. Hassell in 1822 when the house was surrounded by fields.

137 Ashley House, *c.*1990.

138 Nos. 127 and 129 High Street, late 18th-century houses including the original double-bowed shop front.

Some of the Grade II Buildings of Epsom

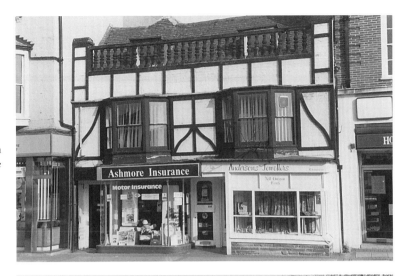

139 Nos. 119 and 121 High Street, houses built in the late 17th century.

140 No. 18 Church Street, a late 17th-century house. From 1755 until recent times it was the Vicarage.

141 The *Old King's Head* public house in Church Street is mid-17th-century.

142 The Grove House, The Grove. A house built in the late 18th century. A house on this site in 1755 was owned by Frederick, 6th Lord Baltimore. Since Woodcote Park Mansion was being rebuilt at that time it is possible that Lord Baltimore was staying at The Grove House.

143 Woodcote House, Woodcote Green. A building that was for many years the home of the Northey family, who were lords of the manor of Cheam, Cuddington and Ewell. The present building dates from the early 19th century and it replaced a house built about one hundred years earlier by Sir Edward Northey, who was Attorney General to William III, Queen Anne and George I. It was his son Edward who acquired the lordship of the manors in 1755. The last Northey to live at Woodcote House was Major General Sir Edward Northey, who sold it in 1939. It is now divided into flats.

144 The Clock House, Dorking Road. A house built in the early part of the 19th century by Sir James Alexander on the site of an earlier building which formed part of The Elms estate and which was visited by Celia Fiennes in about 1712. She described the house and gardens in which she said there were ice houses in mounds at either end of a pond. An ice house, which is of the cup and dome type, remains at the north end of the pond.

Chapter Thirteen

Some People of Epsom

Many interesting people have lived in Epsom and the following is a selection of brief accounts of them in chronological order.

John Toland

John Toland was born near Londonderry in 1670. A college education in Glasgow followed by study at Edinburgh, Leyden and Oxford made him a notable scholar who claimed to know 10 languages. He became a free-thinker quite early, and in 1696 at the age of 26 wrote a book called *Christianity not Mysterious* that challenged the orthodox religious views of the day: the House of Commons voted that the book should be burnt by the common hangman and the author arrested. However, he escaped arrest by finding himself some powerful patrons, such as the Duke of Newcastle, and spending much time abroad on diplomatic missions. He wrote many religious and political pamphlets.

Around 1710 Toland retired for a period to Woodcote-Green, Epsom, which he regarded as 'a refuge from the toil, the noise and impertinence of the world'. He wrote a lengthy account of the town in the form of a letter to a lady friend he addressed as Eudoxa, in which he expressed the delights of living surrounded by beautiful scenery, yet having the diversions of the spa and the convenience of being within easy reach of London. He referred to the town as such an agreeable mixture of trees and buildings that seen from the Downs it was difficult to say whether 'it be a town in a wood, or a wood in a town'. From about 1718 Toland lived at Putney and died in 1722.

145 John Toland, who lived in Epsom for several years following 1710 and wrote a vivid description of the life of the time in 'Letter to Eudoxa.'

Mrs. Mapp, the bone-setter

In the second quarter of the 18th century there practised in Epsom a notorious bone-setter, or shape-mistress as she was sometimes known. I will not offend modern practitioners by calling her an osteopath. She was Sarah Wallin, the daughter of a bone-setter of Hindon in Wiltshire, but she was generally known as Crazy Sally on account of her eccentric behaviour. She is said to have left home because of a family quarrel and, after wandering from place to place, settled in Epsom. In spite of her outrageous ways she acquired a remarkable reputation for her ability to deal with fractured and dislocated limbs. In the words of a contemporary account:

> The cures of the woman bone-setter of Epsom are too many to be enumerated; her band-ages are extraordinary neat and her dexterity in reducing dislocation and setting fractured bones wonderful. The lame come to her daily and she gets a great deal of money, persons of quality who attend her operations making her presents.'

According to a contemporary poem:

146 Mrs. Sara Mapp, more commonly known as Crazy Sally, made a reputation as a bone-setter. The picture comes from an engraving by Hogarth which showed Sara with a number of physicians of the day.

Madam performs her work by pulling, hauling,
And graces all with cursing and with bawling,
The apparatus made with oaths and din,
The bones pulled sometimes out and some-times in.

So great was Sally's renown that she is said to have been offered 100 guineas to spend another year in Epsom. She was strong enough to set any man's dislocated shoulder without assistance. Once, some surgeons who doubted her skill sent along an imposter who pretended that his wrist was out of joint. Finding it was not, she gave it a wrench which did put it out and told him 'to go to the fools who sent you to set it again, or come back this day month and I will do it!'

In 1736, when her reputation was at its height, she married Hill Mapp, a footman to a mercer of Ludgate Hill, in spite of warnings from her friends that it was an unsuitable match. It turned out that they were right: after a fort-night Mapp left her, taking most of her money. She left Epsom and set up business in Pall Mall, but did not prosper there. On 10 December 1737 she died in lodgings at Seven Dials, so miserably poor that the parish had to bury her.

Martin Madan

Martin Madan, who was born in 1726, spent the last ten years or so of his life in Epsom, living at Woodcote End House. Although after Oxford he was called to the bar, he had a reputation for being a bit of a tear-away. He went to hear Wesley preach in order to ridicule him; however, he was so impressed by what he heard that he repented and took holy orders.

He was appointed chaplain to the Lock Hospital near Hyde Park Corner, where his sermons attracted so many people that they had to build a larger chapel. He travelled around preaching and was described as a Genteel Methodist. Madan wrote lots of religious tracts and hymns, including *Hark the herald angels sing*. In 1780 he published a work that he described as 'A Treatise on Female Ruin', which was something a bit unusual at that time because it advocated polygamy, which he argued was supported by the laws of Moses, and would put an end to prostitution. Not many others saw it that way, and there was such a storm of indignation that Madan resigned his chaplaincy at the Lock Hospital and retired into private life at Epsom. The publication was a curious misjudgement by Madan, who seems otherwise to have been a conventional Methodist. His views didn't stop him being made a Justice of the Peace, and in that capacity he distinguished himself by clamping down on illegal games in Epsom during race week. As a result he was burnt in effigy in the High Street. He died in 1790.

The Rev. John Parkhurst

John Parkhurst made sufficient mark as a biblical scholar to be given an entry in the *Dictionary of National Biography*. He was born in 1728 and was educated at Rugby School and Cambridge, being awarded his M.A. in 1752. He was elected a fellow of Clare Hall.

John Parkhurst's father, also John, owned two considerable estates, Catesby in Northamptonshire and Epsom Manor. The future biblical scholar was intended for the church, but he preferred to follow a studious life rather than become a vicar with a parish to look after. His first important work, *A Hebrew and English Lexicon*, was published in 1762 and ran to several editions. In 1769 appeared his *Greek and English Lexicon to the New Testament*, to which was prefixed 'a plain and easy Greek grammar'. This also was well received and he produced further enlarged editions, as well as other scholarly religious works.

When John Parkhurst's father died in 1765 the estates went to trustees for his wife Ricarda and, when she died five years later, they were for the most part sold off and the proceeds divided among her three sons. Epsom Court, the old manor house, was not sold but went to the Rev. John Parkhurst, together with the advowson and great tithes of St Martin's church.

In 1754 John Parkhurst married Susanna Myster, daughter of John Myster of The Cedars, Epsom. She died in 1759, leaving him a daughter and two sons and in 1761 he married Millicent Northey, by whom he had one daughter, who married a Rev. Joseph Thomas. She was well educated by the standards of the day and was able to complete work left unfinished when her father died in 1797.

John Parkhurst was described as rather below the middle size but remarkably upright and firm in his gait. He was of sociable manners and a good conversationalist, although he shunned public occasions.

Frederick Calvert, 6th Lord Baltimore

Born in 1731, Frederick Calvert became the 6th Lord Baltimore on the death of his father in 1751. He inherited the Woodcote Park Estate, Epsom, which had been passed on to the 3rd Lord Baltimore in 1692 on the death of Mrs. Richard Evelyn. Frederick acquired not only Woodcote Park but also the whole of the colony of Maryland in America, which had been granted to the Lords Baltimore by Charles I.

Some of the early Lords Baltimore had been active in founding and administering Maryland, but the 6th Lord had little interest in the province beyond drawing large revenues, and he never visited it. He did, however, travel widely on the Continent and in the Near East with an entourage that included two black eunuchs and eight women. The famous guide to antiquities, Johann Winckelmann, would have nothing to do with the noble lord, whom he considered to have lost all moral and physical taste.

Frederick was the author of several travel books that included *Select pieces of Oriental Wit, Poetry and Wisdom*, which a critic of the day said no more deserved to be published than the author's bills on the road for post-horses. Baltimore's reputation for loose living was not improved when in 1768 he was tried for rape at Kingston Assizes.

The alleged victim was a 26-year-old milliner, Miss Sarah Woodcock, who kept a little shop near the Tower of London. According to the evidence given in court, a gentlewoman came into the shop and persuaded Sarah to go with her on a visit to a lady who wished to buy millinery. They drove in a fine coach to a magnificent house where she was introduced to a man whom she recognised as one who had entered her shop a week earlier and asked her to go with him to a play, an offer she had refused. She immediately asked to be taken home, but was imprisoned in the house for several days, during which the man she later learned was Lord Baltimore made several attempts to rape her, which she fought off. She was then taken by coach out into the country to a large house she knew was near

147   Frederick Calvert, 6th and last Lord Baltimore, who lost his reputation following a trial for rape in 1768. From a painting by Johann Ludwig Tietz.

Epsom from catching sight of a sign-post. There eventually Baltimore had his way with her, in spite of her struggles and cries: he complained that he had never heard such a noise in his life.

After several days at Woodcote Park Sarah was driven back to the London house. She managed to get a message to someone through a window and, in consequence, Sir John Fielding's men, the Bow Street Runners, arrived: Sarah was taken to a magistrate and questioned. At the trial Lord Baltimore's defence was that Miss Woodcock had not been forcibly detained: she had been quite cheerful for much of the time. He was not helped by his witnesses being a thoroughly disreputable bunch, one of whom had himself been fined and imprisoned for an attempted rape. However, Baltimore and those accused of aiding and abetting him were acquitted, largely on the grounds that Sarah could have tried harder to escape.

Although he was acquitted on the rape charge, Lord Baltimore's reputation suffered so severely from the revelations of his reprehensible lifestyle that he sold Woodcote Park and went to live abroad. He died at Naples in 1771 and was brought back to England to be buried in the family vault at Epsom.

Jonathan Boucher

In St Martin's Church, Epsom, there is a bust of Jonathan Boucher, who was vicar of Epsom from 1785 to 1804. He was born in 1738 into a Scottish border family and had a hard childhood because his family had been ruined by the Jacobite Rebellion. However, he acquired sufficient education to be able to get a job at the age of 21 as a tutor in Virginia, although he soon came back to England to take holy orders. He then returned to America where he ran a private school and a plantation as well as being a priest.

Boucher was unpopular in America because of his lack of sympathy for the American revolutionaries and, when the War of Independence started in 1775, he returned to this country. Ten years later he was given the living of Epsom by John Parkhurst and made his mark by amassing a large library and writing several scholarly works, including one on the American Revolution. He died a respected and affluent cleric. As his memorial tablet records: 'The Lord gave him twice as much as he had before; and blessed his latter end more than his beginning.' After his death he was referred to in the Vestry minutes as 'that learned and exemplary divine'.

Boucher was married three times, but it could not be said that he was uncritical of women. In his autobiography he wrote about his third wife whom he outlived: 'Her greatest defect was that her mind was only faintly imbued with a sense of religion. Yet she was really and substantially a good woman and had no foul and unsubdued passions. However, she had contracted habits of indolence: I never saw any person sleep so much and stir so little.'

Lord Lyttelton at Pitt Place

Until 1967 there stood in Church Street, Epsom, near St Martin's Church, Pitt Place, a one time farmhouse that was converted to a mansion around 1770 by Thomas, Lord Lyttelton. It contained stonework from Nonsuch Palace that had been transferred to the building when The Durdans mansion, in which it had been incorporated, was demolished.

Thomas, the 2nd Baron Lyttelton, born in 1744, resided at Pitt Place when he was not in London, where he made some effective speeches in the House of Lords. He was commonly called the wicked Lord Lyttelton because of the extent to which he indulged in all the fashionable vices. He appeared to repent before his marriage at the age of 28, but soon afterwards he deserted his wife for a barmaid whom he carried off to Paris.

It is on record that one night in 1778 at his house in Hill Street, Berkeley Square, Lyttelton dreamed that a bird flew into the room and changed into a woman whom he recognised as one whose daughters he had seduced. The ghostly figure warned him that

148 Jonathan Boucher, who was vicar of Epsom from 1785 to 1804. This shows him *c.*1782.

he would die before midnight three days hence. On the morning of the third day he said he felt very well and believed he would 'bilk the ghost'. He remarked to a friend on the number of 'vulgar fellows' who died at five and thirty (his own age), adding, 'But you and I, who are gentlemen, shall live to a good old age'. The same day, accompanied by acquaintances, he drove to Pitt Place, where he dined and passed a cheerful evening in apparently good health. However, shortly after getting into bed at a quarter past eleven, he had a fit and died.

Some time after the event the artist John Constable stayed at Pitt Place and was told about it. He wrote some notes in which he recorded that Lord Lyttelton died precisely at the hour foretold, 'even though they put the clock forward'.

149 Pitt Place, a one-time farmhouse in Church Street that was converted into a mansion around 1770 by Thomas, Lord Lyttelton. It was demolished in 1967 in spite of two building preservation orders. The mansion had contained stonework that came from the Durdans mansion that was demolished *c.*1750 and which had come originally from Nonsuch Palace.

150   Interior of Pitt Place.

Benjamin Bockett

Benjamin Bockett was vicar of the parish from 1839 to 1883 and it is clear from the Vestry minutes that his relations with the Vestry were not always harmonious.

In 1842 there were complaints that he was asking excessive fees for the erection of tombstones, leading the Vestry to resolve to refer the matter to the Bishop and that, if he should refuse to protect the Parishioners, 'a subscription be entered into to purchase a burial ground for Epsom and its vicinity by which all extortionate fees will be avoided and that it be distinctly understood that the highly respectable body of Dissenters of this Parish be allowed to bury therein according to their own rights.'

There were also arguments with the vicar over who should pay the organist and a threat that, if he did not agree, the churchwardens would be directed to sell the organ. The vicar was censured for not devoting as much time to visiting the sick as had previous vicars.

Benjamin Bradney Bockett was no stranger to controversy: he is reported to have said, 'I am the three B's you know, and a stinging bee too, sometimes, they tell me'. When the bishop threatened to suspend him after numerous complaints, he replied: 'My dear Lord Bishop, if you suspend me, I'll be hanged.'

The following advertisement, characteristic of Bockett, appeared in *The Guardian* on 26 October 1881: 'Curate wanted for Epsom by decided Protestant free from Ritualistic follies. Gown used in pulpit. No intoning, no blasphemous hymns, no eastward position.'

Mrs. Beeton

Chapter Eleven refers to the Dorling family and the children who lived in the grandstand, one of whom was Isabella Mayson, Henry Dorling's stepdaughter, born in 1836. She was nine when she started living in the grandstand; later, she was sent away to a boarding school in Heidelberg, where she had a sound education that included learning German and French and how to make pastry. In July 1856 she married a young

151 Benjamin Bradney Bockett was vicar of Epsom from 1849 to 1883. Copyright: Surrey History Service.

publisher, Samuel Beeton, who had had an early success with the first English edition of *Uncle Tom's Cabin*, by Harriet Beecher Stowe. The wedding breakfast was in the grandstand. Isabella worked with Sam and wrote for him a book on *Household Management* which became the basis of the many editions of Mrs. Beeton that have since appeared. Generations of girls have profited from the book: in the words of a writer in 1907, 'even the writers of romances of domestic life have recorded how it constantly rescues young housekeepers from perplexity and woe'.

Isabella Beeton did not have long to enjoy her success: in 1865 she died of puerperal fever after giving birth to her fourth child. The first two had died in infancy, in spite of the advice on child care given in Isabella's *Household Management*. She packed a great deal into her 29 years: she even found time to organise a mammoth charity campaign to help Lancashire cotton workers who became unemployed as a result of the disruption at the time of the American Civil War.

Archibald Primrose, the 5th Earl of Rosebery

Epsom's Lord Rosebery had a good start in life: his father was the 4th Earl Rosebery and his mother was the only daughter of Earl Stanhope. A tutor at Eton said, 'he was surely the wisest boy that ever lived'. However, he left Oxford without a degree: he was sent down for buying a racehorse and entering it for The Derby, which the authorities took exception to.

Archibald Primrose succeeded to the title in 1868 at the age of 20 on the death of his grandfather, his father having died in 1850. With the title went Dalmeny Park near Edinburgh and other extensive properties in Scotland. In 1878 his marriage to Hannah, only daughter of Baron de Rothschild, brought him the great estate of Mentmore in Buckinghamshire and the associated racehorse stud. Sadly, Hannah died at Dalmeny in 1890, after the unseen hound of Rosebery family myth had been heard baying in the night, as it was believed to do when misfortune was coming

to the Laird. It was a great blow to Rosebery: for the rest of his life he used writing paper with a black border.

Rosebery was drawn into politics as a Liberal when he allowed William Gladstone to use Dalmeny as his headquarters in 1879 in his campaign to secure Midlothian. He soon won respect as a public speaker and two years later was appointed Under-Secretary at the Home Office in charge of Scottish business in the House of Lords. The British Empire became a subject of special concern for Rosebery, and he is thought to have been the first to use the term 'Commonwealth'. He worked also for reform in the House of Lords, although his most significant appointment was that of Foreign Secretary in Gladstone's administration of 1886. In 1894 Prime Minister Gladstone resigned over a disagreement on naval estimates, and Queen Victoria, acting on her own initiative, offered the premiership to Rosebery. Not much more than a year later his government was defeated by a narrow margin on a bill relating to armaments, and he at once resigned

152 Lord Rosebery in about 1869.

153 Lord Rosebery in about 1914.

154 Rosebery's evening ride to combat insomnia would usually be in this carriage.

as Prime Minister and soon after as leader of the Liberal Party. After making his farewell speech he noted in his diary, 'Home to supper. What a relief!'

Ladas, the horse that led to Rosebery being sent down from Oxford, came last in The Derby in a field of 22, but when he started to build up his own stable he began to have a few successes. He acquired Durdans at Epsom in 1874 and started a stud there, but after his marriage the Durdans stud was combined with that at Mentmore. The highlight of his racing was in 1894 when he was Prime Minister and won The Derby with his horse Ladas II. He won again in 1895 with Sir Visto, and yet again in 1905 with Cicero.

When Rosebery bought Durdans he had been mainly attracted by its proximity to Epsom racecourse—the paddock was on his land—but the town of Epsom clearly had a strong hold on his affections. He became an active member of Epsom Urban District Council and supported many local organisations. In 1913 he bought what is now Rosebery Park and gave it to the Council. Rosebery suffered a great deal from insomnia, something that had begun to trouble him as early as 1884. In consequence of his sleeplessness, he would frequently be taken for a drive in the early morning or in the evening. In his later years, Rosebery lived almost con-

tinuously at Durdans, spending less time at Dalmeny and Mentmore.

Rosebery's favourite son was Neil, who, after a spell in the army, was elected M.P. for Wisbech and soon rose to government office. When the First World War came, Neil did not wish to stay in the political arena while his friends were risking their lives abroad. He rejoined the Bucks Yeomanry and was killed on active service at Gaza in Palestine in November 1917. Rosebery was shattered: just a year after his son's death he had a stroke from which he was unconscious during the night of 11 November, Armistice Day. He made a partial recovery, but was left disabled and scarcely able to write with his own hand. He died at Durdans on 21 May 1929 and was taken home to Dalmeny and buried in the little church there.

Rosebery has been described as of middle height, strongly built, with rather prominent light blue eyes and of a nervously impulsive nature. Although at school and university he was not regarded as a brilliant scholar, he showed a great love of the classics and read widely. He wrote biographies of political figures: his life of William Pitt, published in 1891, met with wide approval and was followed by many more similar studies of which that of Lord Randolph Churchill is considered to have been the most successful, notable for its lightness and charm. It has been suggested that literature and historical writing suffered a great loss when the author gave himself over to a political career.

James Chuter Ede

James Ede, always known as Chuter Ede in recognition of his mother's family name, was born in Epsom in 1882 and began his education at the West Hill Infants School followed by the Epsom National School. Later education included periods at Dorking High School, Battersea Pupil Teachers' Centre and two years at Cambridge University. He worked as an assistant master in a number of Surrey elementary schools before service in the army in the First World War.

155 James Chuter Ede, Home Secretary 1945-51, served as a sergeant in the East Surrey Regiment in the First World War.

Chuter Ede had shown an interest in politics before the war and as soon as it was over became active at a local, county and national level. He was the Labour M.P. for South Shields from 1929 to his retirement in 1964. His work with Epsom Urban District Council culminated in his appointment as Charter Mayor when Epsom and Ewell became a borough in 1937. As Chairman of Surrey County Council he had a big impact on education, health and conservation. He worked for public ownership of Walton Downs and Nonsuch Park.

As Parliamentary Secretary in the Ministry of Education, Chuter Ede helped bring the 1944 Education Act to the Statute book and in 1945 was appointed Home Secretary, a position he held until 1951. In this period of office he sponsored dozens of the major bills that were necessary to deal with the backlog of legislation that had accumulated during the War, as well as being responsible for the day-to-day running of the Home Office. One decision was to haunt him: he had refused an appeal against the death sentence for murder by Timothy Evans, only to believe later in his innocence. It brought him to change his mind about the death penalty, which he had previously supported.

When James Ede was made a life peer in 1964 it was as Baron Chuter Ede. He died in 1965 and his funeral service at Epsom Parish Church was attended by many famous politicians. He was buried in the family grave in Epsom Cemetery. Chuter Ede has been described as a popular and well-rounded personality: one of his passions was horse-racing.

Tom Walls

Although Tom Kirby Walls lived in Ewell, rather than Epsom, his association with The Derby justifies his inclusion. He was born in 1883 at Kingsthorpe, Northampton and was educated at Northampton County School. He did not wish to follow his father's trade as a plumber: engine-driving was more to his liking, but he attempted to drive a locomotive before he was trained and he lost his job. This was followed by a year in Canada and a short period in the Metropolitan Police. But the stage called him and he joined a pierrot troupe at Brighton, the start of a career that was to take him through musical comedy to the West End stage, where he specialised in eccentric old gentlemen.

In 1922 he was in a very successful farce with Leslie Henson and this led to a string of farces at the Aldwych Theatre written by Ben Travers, and supported by Ralph Lynn and Robertson Hare. They were phenomenally popular as were the screen comedies that Walls appeared in later. The wealth his work brought enabled him to indulge in a passion for horse-racing: he was able to set up racing stables adjoining his house in Reigate Road, Ewell, with as many as 25 horses in training. Results were not spectacular until 1932, when his horse April the Fifth won the Derby. Walls' last stage appearance was in 1948, by which time his popularity was on the wane, and his income insufficient to support his extravagant life-style: the horses had to be sold. When Tom Walls died in 1949 he was broke. In accordance with his wishes his ashes were scattered over the Derby course.

George Woodcock

George Woodcock, a notable General Secretary of the Trades Union Congress, was born in Lancashire in 1904 where he was educated at a Roman Catholic Elementary School until at the age of 13 he left for employment as a weaver. He became a minor official in the Bamber Bridge and District Weavers' Union, and worked for a TUC scholarship to Ruskin College, Oxford. This he won, and further study at New College, Oxford led to a first class degree in philosophy, politics and economics in 1933.

Woodcock joined the TUC as head of the Research and Economic Department in 1936 after a period in the Civil Service and worked closely with the General Secretary,

156 George Woodcock was a notable General Secretary of the Trades Union Congress.

Walter Citrine, who later became Lord Citrine. In 1947 he was appointed Assistant General Secretary and 1960 saw his promotion to General Secretary, a position he held with distinction until his retirement in 1969.

Before and after his retirement from the TUC, George Woodcock served on numerous commissions relating to economics and industrial relations, and his work was recognised by the award of honorary degrees by a number of universities. The City of London made him a freeman in 1965 and two years later the Queen appointed him a Privy Councillor. He had been made a CBE in 1953.

Woodcock was well aware of the delicate balance that had to be found between free trade unions and economic stability with low inflation. He advocated policies aimed at maintaining a high rate of employment and could see that trade unions had to accept wage restraints to enable a government to follow such policies. He argued his case with passion and an expressiveness in which his large bushy eyebrows would play a full part: they were a gift to cartoonists.

George Woodcock lived in Lower Hill Road, Epsom, from 1960-79 with his wife Laura Mary, who played a prominent part in the life of the town as a magistrate, councillor, alderman and mayor. She was the first woman to be made a Freeman of Epsom. The couple had two children, a son and a daughter. George Woodcock died in 1979.

Frank Hampson, the creator of Dan Dare

Frank Hampson, the strip cartoonist who created the hugely popular Dan Dare, Chief Pilot of the Interplanet Space Fleet, was born in Manchester in 1918. On leaving school he became a telegraph boy for the Post Office and in his spare time drew comic cartoons and took evening classes in art. He became a civil servant and by 1937 was having comic strips published in the GPO staff magazine. The following year he resigned his job to become a full-time art student, but his studies were interrupted by the outbreak of the Second World War in which he served as a driver in the Royal Army Service Corps before taking a commission.

Frank Hampson was able to continue his studies after demobilisation in 1946, supported by a grant and helped out with proceeds from freelance work which included doing illustrations for *The Anvil*, a monthly religious magazine that was edited and published by the Rev. Marcus Morris, whose ambition it was to publish for boys a weekly comic based on Christian principles as an alternative to the crime and horror comics flooding in from America. The new comic which they called *Eagle* was taken up by Sir Edward Hulton, publisher of *Picture Post*, and the first edition appeared on 14 April 1950 at a price of 4d.

Eagle was an instant success, largely because of the work put into it by Frank Hampson. He was responsible for the layout as well as writing and drawing all the principal strips. It was a striking creation: a tabloid comic printed in full colour. The front page featured the serial that above all others became associated with *Eagle*, 'Dan Dare, Pilot of the Future'. By 1955 the art work was being produced in Hampson's house in College Avenue, Epsom, where studios and a dark room had been set up for Hampson and the team working on the publication. The work was meticulous: scale models of space craft were constructed so that they could be accurately drawn from any angle. This attention to detail was invaluable when they began merchandising Dan Dare uniforms, space-ships and ray-guns.

The successful enterprise began to go downhill in 1960, when *Eagle* was sold off to Odham's Press and later to IPC. Frank Hampson left *Eagle* and after a period of ill health worked as a graphics technician at Ewell Technical College (now North East Surrey College of Technology). His work was recognised in 1975 when he was awarded the top award at the International Festival of Comics for a lifetime devoted to comic art. It was said to be the finest seen in post-war children's comics. Frank Hampson died on 8 July 1985 in Epsom Cottage Hospital aged 66.

Bibliography

Andrews, James, *Reminiscences of Epsom* (L.W.Andrew & Son, 1904)

Bailey, W.J., 'The Strowger Automatic Exchange at Epsom' (Post Office Electrical Engineers Journal Vol. 5, 1912)

Bird, J.B. and D.G., ed.,'The Archaeology of Surrey to 1540' (Surrey Archaeological Society, 1987)

Black, E.W., *The Roman Villas of South-East England* (B.A.R., 1987)

Blair, John, *Early Medieval Surrey* (Alan Publishing and Surrey Archaeological Society, 1991)

Boucher, Jonathan, *Reminiscences of an American Loyalist, 1738-1789* (Houghton, Mifflin Co., 1925)

Brayley, Edward Wedlake, *A Topographical History of Surrey* (J.S. Virtue & Co., 1848)

Clark, F.L., 'The History of Epsom Spa', *Surrey Archaeological Collections*, vol. 57 (Surrey Archaeological Society, 1960)

Compton, Alistair, *The Man Who Drew Tomorrow* (Who Dares Publishing, 1985)

Cox, Valerie, 'Epsom & Ewell Cottage Hospital, 1877-1995' (unpublished archive copy, 1995)

Cunningham, Margaret, *The Story of the Oaks and Oaks Park* (Sutton Leisure Services, 1993)

Currie, Christopher K., *An evaluation of the archaeological and historical landscape of Ashtead and Epsom Commons in Surrey* (Historic Countryside Group of Surrey County Council, 1999)

Epsom Common Association, *Epsom Common* (Living History Publications Local Guide No. 5, 1981)

Essen, R.I., *Epsom's Hospital Railway* (Pullingers, 1991)

Essen, R.I., *Epsom's Suffragette* (Pullingers, 1993)

Essen, R.I., *Thirties Epsom* (Pullingers, 1992)

Exwood, Maurice, *Epsom Wells*, Second Edition (Epsom and Ewell Borough Council, 2000)

Foster, James W. and Manakee, Beta K., *The Lords Baltimore* (Enoch Pratt Free Library, Baltimore, 1961)

Freeman, Sarah, *Isabella and Sam* (Victor Gollancz, 1977)

Hampton, J.N., 'Roman Ashtead' in *Ashtead, A Village Transformed* (Leatherhead and District Local History Society, 1977)

The Gentleman's Magazine, Vol. 38, 1768

Home, Gordon, *Epsom, Its History and Surroundings*, 1901 (Republished S.R. Publishers Ltd, 1971)

Hunn, David, *Epsom Racecourse* (Davis-Poynter Ltd., 1993)

Jackson, Harry, *Christ Church Centenary, 1876-1976* (Epsom, 1976)

Lee, William, 'Report on sanitary conditions in the Parish of Epsom' (HMSO, 1849)

Lehmann, H.L., *The Residential Copyholds of Epsom* (Epsom and Ewell Borough Council, 1987)

Lowther, A.W.G., 'Excavations at Ashtead, Surrey', *Surrey Archaeological Collections*, vols.37 and 38 (Surrey Archaeological Society, 1927 and 1930)

Malden, H.E., ed., *The Victoria History of the County of Surrey* (Archibald Constable and Co., 1902)

Manning, O. and Bray, W., *The History and Antiquities of Surrey* (1804-14)

Marquess of Crewe, *Lord Rosebery* (John Murray, 1931)

Marshall, C.F. Dendy, *History of the Southern Railway* (Ian Allan Ltd., 1968)

Morris, Christopher, ed., *The Journeys of Celia Fiennes* (Cresset, 1949)

Nairn, Ian and Pevsner, Nikolaus, *The Buildings of England: Surrey* (Penguin Books Ltd., 1971)

Nonsuch Antiquarian Society Publications, occasional papers: No. 28 'The Administration of Justice in Epsom and Ewell'; No. 30 'The Epsom Vestry'; No. 31 'The Unhealthy State of Epsom in 1849'; No. 35 'The Listed Buildings and Ancient Monuments of Epsom and Ewell'; No. 37 'Waterloo House: The Epsom Spa Assembly Rooms'; No. 38 'Victorian Epsom Revealed through the Census'.

Salter, Brian, J., ed., *Epsom Town, Downs and Common* (Living History Local Guide No. 3, 1976)

Saunders, M. John, 'Late Bronze/Early Iron Age settlement evidence from Manor Hospital, Epsom', *Surrey Archaeological Collections*, vol. 87 (Surrey Archaeological Society, 2000)

Schellinks, William, *Travels in England, 1661-1663*. Translated from the Dutch and edited by Exwood, M. and Lehmann, H.L. (Royal Historical Society, 1993)

Shadwell, Thomas, *Epsom Wells: a Comedy* (London, 1674)

Surrey Record Society, vol. xxvi, *Fitznell's Cartulary* (1968)

Surrey Record Society, vol. xxxiv, *Parson and Parish in Eighteenth-Century Surrey*. Replies to Bishops' Visitations (1994)

Surrey Record Society, vol. xxxv, *The 1851 Religious Census: Surrey* (1997)

Swete, C.J., *Handbook of Epsom* (J. Rowe, 1860)

Tate, W.E., *A Domesday of English enclosure acts and awards* (University of Reading, 1978)

Toland, John, *The Description of Epsom* (London, 1711)

Turner, J.T. Howard, *The London, Brighton and South Coast Railway* (Batsford, 1978)

Turner, Stephen, *Epsom Church* (The British Publishing Company Ltd., 1977)

Valentine, Ruth, *Asylum, Hospital, Haven. A History of Horton Hospital* (Riverside Mental Health Trust, 1996)

White, Reginald, *Ancient Epsom* (William Pile Ltd., 1928)

White, Trevor and Harte, Jeremy, *Epsom: A Pictorial History* (Phillimore, 1992)

White, Trevor, *Epsom Entertained* (T. White, 1989)

White, Trevor, *War-Time in a Surrey Town* (T. White, 1994)

Index

Page numbers in **bold** refer to illustrations or their captions